MY FOUR WEEKS IN FRANCE

MY FOUR WEEKS
IN FRANCE

By

RING W. LARDNER

AUTHOR OF

Gullible's Travels, Etc.

ILLUSTRATED BY

WALLACE MORGAN

INDIANAPOLIS
THE BOBBS-MERRILL COMPANY
PUBLISHERS

PRESS OF
BRAUNWORTH & CO.
BOOK MANUFACTURERS
BROOKLYN, N. Y.

CONTENTS

MY FOUR WEEKS IN FRANCE

MY FOUR WEEKS IN FRANCE

I

DODGING SUBMARINES TO COVER THE BIGGEST GAME OF ALL

Wednesday, July 18. A Lake Michigan Port.

I KEPT an appointment to-day with a gentleman from Somewhere in Connecticut.

"How," said he, "would you like to go to France?"

I told him I'd like it very much, but that I was thirty-two years old, with a dependable wife and three unreliable children.

"Those small details," he said, "exempt you from military duty. But we want you as a war correspondent."

I told him I knew nothing about war. He said it

9

had frequently been proved that that had nothing to do with it. So we hemmed and we hawed, pro and con, till my conscientious objections were all overruled.

"In conclusion," said he, "we'd prefer to have you go on a troopship. That can be arranged through the War Department. There'll be no trouble about it."

Monday, July 30.   A Potomac Port.

To-day I took the matter up with the War Department, through Mr. Creel.

"Mr. Creel," I said, "can I go on a troopship?"

"No," said Mr. Creel.

There was no trouble about it.

Wednesday, August 1.   An Atlantic Port.

The young man in the French Consulate has taken a great fancy to me. He will not visé my passport till I bring him two more autographed pictures of myself.

George W. Gloom of the steamship company said there would be a ship sailing Saturday.

"Are we convoyed through the danger zone?" I inquired.

"We don't guarantee it," said he. "There has never been an accident on this line," he added.

"What I was thinking about," said I, "wouldn't be classed as an accident." Further questioning developed the comforting fact that the ship I am taking has never been sunk.

I told him I wanted a cabin to myself, as I expected to work.

"You will be in with two others," he said.

"I would pay a little more to be alone," said I.

This evidently was not worth answering, so I asked him how long the trip would take.

"I know nothing about it," said he.

"I believe that," said I when I was well out of his ear-shot.

Wednesday, August 8.   At Sea.

We left port at ten last night, a mere three and a half days behind schedule. The ship and I should be very congenial, as we are about the same age.

My roommates are a young man from Harvard

and a young man from Yale, but so far I have managed to keep the conversation neutral. We suspect that they made ours a first-class cabin by substituting the word 1ère for 2ème on the sign, and I am very certain that my berth was designed for Rabbit Maranville.

Our passenger list includes a general, a congressman, a lady novelist and her artist husband, French; a songbird, also French; two or three majors, a Thaw, and numerous gentlemen of the consular service. The large majority on board are young men going into American Ambulance and Y. M. C. A. work.

After breakfast this morning there was life-boat drill, directed by our purser, who is permanently made up as Svengali. He sent us down to our cabins to get our life-belts and then assigned us to our boats. Mine, No. 12, is as far from my cabin as they could put it without cutting it loose from the ship, and if I happen to be on deck when that old torpedo strikes, believe me, I'm not going to do a Marathon for a life-belt. Shoes off, and a running hop, step and jump looks like the best system.

Moreover, I'm going to disobey another of the rules, which is that each passenger must remain calm.

Next we had to fill out a form for the enlightenment of Svengali as to our destination, business, home address, foreign address, literary tastes, etc. One item was "the names of relatives or friends you lofh." This was unanswered, as nobody aboard seemed to know the meaning of the verb.

In the fumoir this afternoon a young American wanted a match. He consulted his dictionary and dug out "allumette." But he thought the *t's* were silent and asked Auguste for "allumay." Auguste disappeared and returned in five minutes with a large glass of lemonade. The cost of that little French lesson was two francs.

I am elected to eat at the "second table." Our bunch has luncheon at twelve-thirty and dinner at seven. The first table crowd's hours are eleven and five-thirty. Breakfast is a free-for-all and we sit where we choose. My trough mates at the meals are two Americans, a Brazilian, and four Frenchmen. Ours is a stag table, which unfortunate circumstance is due to the paucity of women, or, as

they are sometimes called, members of the fair sex.
The Brazilian speaks nine or ten languages, but
seems to prefer French. The two Americans are
always engaged in sotto voce dialogue, and the four
Frenchmen race with the Brazilian for the conver-
sational speed championship of the high seas. This
leaves me free to devote all my time to the proper
mastication of food.

Thursday, August 9.   Completely at Sea.

A gentleman on board is supplied with one of
these newfangled one hundred dollar safety suits.
The wearer is supposed to be able to float indefinitely. It is also a sort of thermos bottle, keeping
one warm in cold water and cool in hot. I do not
envy the gent. I have no ambition to float indefinitely. And if I didn't happen to have it on when
the crash came, I doubt whether I could spare the
time to change. And besides, if I ever do feel that
I can afford one hundred dollars for a suit, I won't
want to wear it for the edification of mere fish.

When Svengali isn't busy pursing, he is usually

engaged in chess matches with another of the officers. The rest of the idle portion of the crew stand
round the table and look on. Sometimes they look
on for an hour without seeing a move made, but
they never seem to lose interest. Every little move-
ment brings forth a veritable torrent of français
from the spectators. I can understand the fascina-
tion of chess from the player's end, but could get
few thrills from watching, especially when there
was standing room only.

Far more fascinating to look at is the game two
of my French trough mates play at breakfast. The
rules are simple. You take a muffin about the size
of a golf ball. You drop it into your cup of chocolate. Then you fish for it, sometimes with a spoon,
but more often with your fingers. The object is to
convey it to your mouth without discoloring your
necktie. Success comes three times in five.

The players are about evenly matched. One of
them I suspect, is not in the game for sport's sake,
but has a worthier object. Nature supplied him
with a light gray mustache, and a chocolate brown

would blend better with his complexion. If the muffins hold out, his color scheme will be perfect before we reach port.

The discovery has been made that there's a man on board who plays the cornet, so if we are subbed it will not be an unmitigated evil.

Friday, August 10.

Every morning one sees on the deck people one never saw before, and as we have not stopped at any stations since we started, the inference is that certain parties have not found the trip a continuous joy ride.

A news bulletin, published every morning, sometimes in English and sometimes in French, keeps us right up to date on thrilling events, thrillingly spelled. I have copied a sample:

It is now the tim for the final invaseon of the west by the eastren american league teams and before this clash is over it will be definitively known wether the two sox teams are to fight it out in a nip and tuk finish or wether the Chicago sox will have a comfortable margen to insure a world series betwean the two largest American citys Chicago and New York.

The French news deals exclusively with the developments in the world series Over There, which is, perhaps, almost as important.

A new acquaintance made to-day was that of the Gentleman from Louisiana. He introduced himself to scold me and another guy for not taking sufficient exercise. We told him we found little pleasure in promenading the deck.

"That's unnecessary," he said. "Get yourselves a pair of three-pound dumb-bells and use them a certain length of time every day."

So we are constantly on the lookout for a dumb-bell shop, but there seems to be a regrettable lack of such establishments in mid-ocean.

The Gentleman from Louisiana says he is going to join the Foreign Legion if they'll take him. He is only seventy years old.

"But age makes no difference to a man like I," says he. "I exercise and keep hard. All my friends are hard and tough. Why, one of my friends, an undertaker, always carries a razor in his boot."

Presumably this bird never allows psychological depression in his business.

The Gentleman from Louisiana continues:

"I've got a reputation for hardness, but I'm only hard when I know I'm right. I used such hard language once that they injected me from a committee. I was state senator then. But in all the time I held office I never talked more than two minutes."

We expressed polite regret that he was not a state senator still. And we asked him to have a lemonade.

"No, thank you. Even the softest drinks have a peculiar effect on me. They make my toes stick together."

We guaranteed to pry those members apart again after he had quenched his thirst, but he would not take a chance.

On the way cabinward from this fascinating presence, I was invited into a crap game on the salle à manger floor. The gentleman with the dice tossed a hundred-franc note into the ring and said: "Shoot it all." And the amount was promptly oversubscribed. So I kept on going cabinward.

Samedi, 11 Août.

The man back there in the steamship office can no more truthfully say: "There has never been an accident on this line."

I awoke at three-thirty this morning to find the cabin insufferably hot and opened the port-hole which is directly above my berth. The majority of the ocean immediately left its usual haunts and came indoors. Yale and Harvard were given a shower bath and I had a choice of putting on the driest things I could find and going on deck or drowning where I lay. The former seemed the preferable course.

Out there I found several fellow voyagers asleep in their chairs and a watchman in a red-and-white tam-o'-shanter scanning the bounding main for old Hans W. Periscope.

I wanted sympathy, but the watchman informed me that he ne comprended pas anglais, monsieur. So we stood there together and scanned, each in his own language.

My garçon de cabine promises he will have me thoroughly bailed out by bedtime to-night.

I sat at a different breakfast table, but there was no want of entertainment. At my side was a master of both anglais and français, and opposite him an American young lady who thinks French is simply just impossible to learn.

"Mademoiselle," says he, "must find it difficult to get what she likes to eat."

"I certainly do," says she. "I don't understand a word of what's on the menu card."

"Perhaps I can help mademoiselle," says he. "Would she like perhaps a grapefruit?"

She would and she'd also like oatmeal and eggs and coffee. So he steered her straight through the meal with almost painful politeness, but in the intervals when he wasn't using his hands as an aid to gallant discourse, he was manicuring himself with a fork.

This afternoon they drug me into a bridge game. My partner was our congressman's secretary. Our opponents were a Standard Oil official and a vice-consul bound for Italy. My partner's middle name

The majority of the ocean immediately left its usual haunts and came indoors

was Bid and Mr. Oil's was Double. And I was too
shy to object when they said we'd play for a cent a
point.

At the hour of going to press, Standard Oil had
practically all the money in the world. And my
partner has learned that a holding of five clubs
doesn't demand a bid of the same amount.

Sunday, August 12.

The boat seems to be well supplied with the
necessities of life, such as cocktails and cards and
chips, but it is next to impossible to obtain luxuries
like matches, ice-water and soap.

Yale and Harvard both knew enough to bring
their own soap, but my previous ocean experiences
were mostly with the Old Fall River Line, on which
there wasn't time to wash. Neither Yale nor Harvard ever takes a hint. And "Apportez-moi du
savon, s'il vous plaît," to the cabin steward is just
as ineffectual.

All good people attended service this morning,
and some bad ones played poker this afternoon.

In a burst of generosity I invited a second-class

French young lady of five summers to have some candy. She accepted, and her acceptance led to the discovery that the ship's barber is also its candy salesman.

This barber understands not a syllable of English, which fact has added much to young America's enjoyment. The boys, in the midst of a hair cut, say to him politely: "You realize that you're a damn rotten barber?" And he answers smilingly: "Oui, oui, monsieur." Yesterday, I am told, a young shavee remarked: "You make me sick." The barber replied as usual, and the customer was sick all last night.

To-morrow afternoon there is to be a "concert" and I'm to speak a piece, O Diary!

Monday, August 13.

The concert was "au profit du Secours National de France. Œuvre fondée pour répartir les Secours aux Victimes de la Guerre."

Ten minutes before starting time they informed me that I was to talk on "The American National Game," and I don't even know how the White Sox came out a week ago to-morrow.

The afternoon's entertainment opened with a few well-chosen remarks by our congressman. The general, designated on the program as "chairman," though his real job was toastmaster, talked a while about this, that and the other thing, and then introduced the cornet player, using his real name. This gentleman and I blew at the same time, so I have no idea what he played. I got back in time for some pretty good harmonizing by three young Americans and a boy from Cincinnati. Then there was a Humorous Recitation (the program said so) by a gent with a funny name, and some really delightful French folk songs by the lady novelist. After which came a Humorous Speech (the program forgot to say so) by myself, necessarily brief, as I gave it in French. The French songbird followed with one of those things that jump back and forth between Pike's Peak and the Grand Cañon, and a brave boy played a ukelele, and the quartette repeated. In conclusion, we all rose and attempted *La Marseillaise.*

Some of the programs had been illustrated by the lady novelist's artist husband, and these were auctioned off after the show. I made my financial contribution indirectly, through better card players than myself. My bridge partner, I noticed, had recovered from his attack of the Bids.

Tuesday, August 14.

The concert, by the way, was given in the salon de conversation, which, I think, should be reserved for the Gentleman from Louisiana. He has now told me two hundred times that he won his election to the State Senate by giving one dollar and a half to "a nigger."

One of our young field-service men spoiled the forenoon poker game with a lecture on how to catch sharks. His remarkable idea is to put beefsteak on a stout copper wire and troll with it. He has evidently been very intimate with this family of fish, and he says they are simply crazy about beefsteak. Personally, I have no desire to catch sharks. There are plenty aboard. But I do wish he had not got to the most interesting part of his theory at the moment the dealer slipped me four sixes before the draw. Everybody was too busy listening to stay.

We have discovered that the man behind the gun in the fumoir bears a striking resemblance to Von Hindenburg, but no one has been found who will tell him so.

There was a track meet this afternoon, and the author of this diary was appointed referee. But the first event, a wheelbarrow race, was so exciting that he feared for his weak heart and resigned in favor of our general. There didn't seem to be much else to the meet but ju-jutsu, the sport in which skill is supposed to triumph over brawn. I noticed that a two-hundred-and-thirty-pound man was the winner.

We are in that old zone, and the second table's dinner hour has been advanced to half past six so that there need be no lights in the dining-room. Also, we are ordered not to smoke, not even to light a match, on deck after dark. The fumoir will be running for the last time, but the port-holes in it will all be sealed, meaning that after thirty-five smokers have done their best for a few hours the atmosphere will be intolerable. We can stay on deck smokeless, or we can try to exist in the airless

fumoir, or we can go to bed in the dark and wish
we were sleepy. And the worst is yet to come.

Wednesday, August 15.

The rules for to-night and to-morrow night provide for the closing of our old friend, the fumoir,
at seven o'clock, and that witching hour is on you
long before you expect it, for they jump the clock
fifteen minutes ahead every time it's noon or midnight. The ship will not be lit up. The passengers
may, if they do their shopping early.

There was another life-boat "drill" this afternoon. Every one was required to stand in front of
his canoe and await the arrival of Svengali. When
that gent appeared, he called the roll. As soon as
you said "Here" or "Present," your part of the
"drill" was over. When the time comes I must do
my drifting under an alias, as Svengali insists on
designating me as Monsieur Gardnierre. But No.
12 is at least honored with two second-class ladies.
Many a poor devil on the ship is assigned to a life-
boat that is strictly stag.

The Gentleman from Louisiana to-day sprang
this one:

"You know when I part my hair in the middle I look just like a girl. Well, sir, during the Mardi Gras, two years ago, I put on a page's costume and parted my hair in the middle. And you know girls under a certain age must go home at nine o'clock in the evening. Well, sir, a policeman accosted me and told me I had to go home. I gave him the bawling out of his life. And maybe you think he wasn't surprised!"

Maybe I do think so.

The Gentleman strayed to the subject of Patti and wound up with a vocal imitation of that lady. He stopped suddenly when his voice parted in the middle.

We have seen no periscopes, but when I opened my suit-case this morning I met face to face one of those birds that are house pets with inmates of seven-room flats at twenty-five dollars per month. I missed fire with a clothes brush, and before I could aim again he had submerged under a vest. Looks as if the little fellow were destined to go with me to Paris, but when I get him there I'll get him good.

Thursday, August 16.

Great excitement last night when a small un-lighted boat was sighted half a mile or so off our port. Our gunners, who are said to receive a bonus for every effective shot, had the range all figured out when the pesky thing gave us a signal of friend-ship. It may have been part of the entertainment.

To-day we persuaded the Gentleman from Lou-isiana to part his hair in the middle. The New Orleans policeman is not guilty.

It develops that while first- and second-class pas-sengers were unable to read or smoke after dark, the third-class fumoir is running wide open and the Greeks have their cigarettes, libations and card games, while the idle rich bore one another to death with conversation.

Un Américain aboard is now boasting of the world's championship as a load carrier. It was too much trouble for him to pay Auguste for each beverage as it was served, so he ran a two days' charge account. His bill was one hundred and seventy-eight francs, or thirty-five dollars and sixty cents.

"Who got all the drinks?" he asked Auguste.

"You, monsieur," that gent replied.

"And what do you charge for a highball?"

"One franc, monsieur," said Auguste.

Which means, if Auguste is to be believed, that one hundred and seventy-eight highballs went down one throat in two days. And the owner of the throat is still alive and well. Also, he says he will hereafter pay as you enter.

As an appetizer for dinner to-night the captain told everybody to remain on deck, fully dressed and armed with a life-belt, this evening, until he gave permission to retire.

We're all on deck, and in another minute it will be too dark to write.

To-morrow night, Boche willing, we will be out of the jurisdiction of this Imp of Darkness.

II

I GET TO PARIS AND ENCOUNTER SOME STRANGE SIGHTS

Friday, August 17.   A French Port.

IN obedience to the captain's orders we remained on deck last night, fully dressed, till our ship was past the danger zone and in harbor. There was a rule against smoking or lighting matches, but none against conversation.

The Gentleman from Louisiana and a young American Field Service candidate had the floor. The former's best was a report of what he saw once while riding along beside the Columbia River. An enormous salmon jumped out of the water and raced six miles with the train before being worn out. Whether the piscatorial athlete flew or rode a motor-cycle, we were unable to learn.

The Gentleman from Louisiana yielded to his

younger and stronger countryman. Some one had spoken of the lack of convoy. "Don't you think we haven't a convoy," the kid remarked.

I scanned the sea in all directions and saw nothing but the dark waters. "Where is it?" I inquired.

"There's one on each side of us," said Young America. "They're about twenty miles from the ship."

"I should think," said somebody, "that a very slender submarine might slip in between our side kicks and us and do its regular job."

"No chance," the youth replied. "The convoy boats are used as decoys. The sub would see them first and spend all its ammunition."

A little later he confided in me that the new American war-ships were two hundred and forty-five thousand horsepower. I had no idea there were that many horses left to measure by.

We spotted a shooting star. "That was a big one," I said.

"Big! Do you know the actual size of those things? I got it straight from a professor of astronomy. Listen. They're as small as a grain of sand."

"Why do they look so big?"

"Because they're so far away and they travel so fast."

Round ten o'clock, beckoning lights ashore told us we were close to safety. But the French gunners remained at their posts two hours longer. The captain's shouted order, relieving them from duty, was music to our ears.

After midnight, however, we turned a complete circle, and at once the deck was alive with rumors. We had been hit, we were going to be hit, we were afraid we would be hit, and so on. The fact was that our pilot from ashore was behind time and we circled round rather than stand still and be an easy target while awaiting him. We were in harbor and anchored at three. Many of us stayed up to see the sun rise over France. It was worth the sleep it cost.

They told us we would not dock until six to-night. Before retiring to my cabin for a nap, I heard we had run over a submarine and also that we had not. The latter story lacked heart interest, but had the merit, probably, of truth.   Submarines have little regard for traffic laws, but are careful not to stall their engines in the middle of a boulevard.

I was peacefully asleep when the French officers came aboard to give us and our passports the Double O.   They had to send to my cabin for me. I was ordered to appear at once in the salon de conversation.   A barber hater addressed me through his beard and his interpreter: "What is Monsieur Laudanum's business in France?"

I told him I was a correspondent.

"For who?"

"Mark Sullivan."

"Have you credentials from him?"

"No, sir."

"Your passport says you are going to Belgium. Do you know there are no trains to Belgium?"

"I know nothing about it."

"Well, there are no trains.   How will you go there?"

"I'll try to get a taxi," I said.

"Are you going from here to Paris?"

"Yes."

"And where are you going from Paris?"

"I don't know."

"Please explain that answer."

"I will go wherever the authorities permit me to go."

"That is not a satisfactory answer."

"I'm sorry."

"What is your real business in France?"

"To write."

"I'm afraid we'll have to keep your passport. You will appear to-morrow morning at nine o'clock at this address."

And they handed me a scary-looking card.

On the deck I met our congressman and told him my troubles.

"I know these fellows very well," he said. "If you like, I can fix it for you."

"No," I replied proudly. "I'd rather do my own fixing."

At the dock I got into a taxi and asked to be taken to the —— Hotel. Not to my dying day will I forget that first ride in a French taxi. Part of the time we were on the right side of the street, part of the time on the left, and never once were we traveling under a hundred and fifty miles an hour. We turned twenty corners and always on one ear. We grazed dozens of frightened pedestrians, many of them men crippled in the war, or by taxis, and women too old to dodge quickly. We aimed at a score of rickety horse-drawn vehicles, but our control was bad and we bumped only one. In front of the hostelry we stopped with a jerk.

"Comme beaucoup?" I asked the assassin.

"Un franc cinquante," he said.

Only thirty cents, and I thought I knew why. When they get through a trip without killing any one, they feel they have not done themselves justice nor given you a square deal.

I found myself a seat at a sidewalk table and ordered sustenance. The vial they brought it in was labeled "Bière Ritten," but I suspect the adjective was misspelled.

Till darkness fell I watched the passing show— street-cars with lady motormen and conductors; hundreds of old carts driven by old women, each cart acting as a traveling roof for an old dog;

wounded soldiers walking or hobbling along, some of them accompanied by sad-faced girls; an appalling number of women in black; a lesser number of gayly garbed and extremely cordial ones, and whole flocks of mad taxis, seeking whom they might devour.

By using great caution at the street crossings, I succeeded in reaching the telegraph office where I wrote a message informing Paris friends of my arrival. I presented it to the lady in the cage, who handed it back with the advice that it must be rewritten in French. I turned away discouraged and was starting out again into the gloom when I beheld at a desk the songbird of the ship. Would she be kind enough to do my translating? She would.

The clerk approved the new document, and asked for my passport. I told her it had been taken away. She was deeply grieved, then, but without it monsieur could send no message. Bonne nuit!

Back at the hotel I encountered the Yankee vice-consul, a gentleman from Bedford, Indiana. I told him my sad plight, and he said if matters got too serious his office would undertake to help.

With his assurances to comfort me, I have retired to my room to write, to my room as big as Texas and furnished with all the modern inconveniences.

Saturday, August 18. Paris.

It is Saturday night and they have hot water, but before I take advantage of it I must recount the thrilling experiences of the day.

After a sidewalk breakfast of "oofs" and so-called café in Bordeaux, I went to keep my engagement at court. It was apparent that I was not the only suspect. The walk outside and the room within were crowded with shipmates, most of them from the second cabin, all looking scared to death.

I stood in line till I realized that I must make it snappy if I wanted to catch the eleven-five for Paris; then I butted my way into the august presence of Him of the Beard.

He recognized me at once and told me with his hands to go up-stairs. In a room above I found the English-speaking cross-examiner, with the accent on the cross.

He waved me to a chair and began his offensive.

"Monsieur Laudanum," he said, "when I asked you yesterday how you expected to get to Belgium, you said something about a taxi. That answer was not satisfactory. You have not explained anything to us. I do not believe we can allow you to leave Bordeaux."

"All right, sir." I arose.

"Sit down!" he barked. "Now tell me if you have any explanations to make."

"Nothing beyond what I said yesterday. I have come here to write. I want to go to Paris, and when I arrive there I will find out where else I will be permitted to go."

"It seems very strange to me that you have no papers."

"Yes, sir."

"Have you any?"

I searched my pockets and produced a used-up check book on a Chicago bank. The ogre read every little stub and I felt flattered by his absorbed interest. When he had spent some five minutes on the last one, which recorded a certain painful trans-action between me and a man-eating garage, he returned my book and said: "You don't satisfy me at all. You will have to stay here."

"Suppose," said I, "that the American consul vouches for me."

"That will make no difference. You do not seem to realize that we are at war."

"Not with America."

"I don't know your nationality."

"I thought," said I, "that my passport hinted at it."

"You will have to stay in Bordeaux," was his pertinent reply.

"Thank you, sir," I said, and arose again.

"Sit down," said he, "and wait a minute."

He was out of the room five years.

"If he ever does come back," I thought, "it will be in the company of five or six large gendarmes."

But when he came back he came alone.

"Here," he said abruptly, "is your passport. You will be permitted to go to Paris. We will keep track of you there." And he bowed me out of the joint.

The crowd down-stairs seemed as great as ever,

and as scared. I picked my way through it with my head held high, a free man.

I decided on a fiacre for my trip from hotel to station. It would be safer, I thought. But I learned, on our interminable way, that defensive fighting in the streets of Bordeaux is far more terrifying, far more dangerous than the aggressive taxi kind. We were run into twice and just missed more times than I could count, and besides my conveyance was always on the verge of a nervous breakdown. 'Spite all the talk of periscopes and subs, the journey across the ocean was parlor croquet compared to my fiacre ride in Bordeaux.

While awaiting my turn at the ticket window I observed at the gate a French soldier wearing a large businesslike bayonet. "Probably to punch tickets with," I thought, but was mistaken. Another gentleman attended to that duty, and the soldier did not give me so much as the honor of a glance.

Outside on the platform were a few of the Red Cross and Y. M. C. A. men of our ship, and I learned from them that one of their number had suffered a sadder fate than I. He had tried to get by on a Holland passport, viséed at the French consulate in New York, and been quietly but firmly persuaded ·to take the next boat back home.

I shared a compartment on the train with a native of the Bronx, and a French lady who just couldn't make her eyes behave, and two bored-looking French gentlemen of past middle age, not to mention in detail much more baggage than there was room for. The lady and the two gentlemen wore gloves, which made the Bronxite and me feel very bourgeois.

Our train crew, with the possible exception of the engineer and fireman whom I didn't see, was female, and, thinking I might some time require the services of the porter, I looked in my dictionary for the feminine of George.

To try my knowledge of française, I had purchased at the station a copy of *Le Cri de Paris*. I found that I could read it very easily by consulting the dictionary every time I came to a word.

But the scenery and the people were more interesting than *Le Cri*, the former especially. Perfect automobile roads, lined with trees; fields, and truck gardens in which aged men and women, young girls and little boys were at work; green hills and valleys; winding rivers and brooks, and an occasional château or a town of fascinating architecture—these helped to make us forget the heat and dust of the trip and the ear-splitting shrieks of our engines. No wonder the boche coveted his neighbor's house.

We stopped for some time at one particularly beautiful town and went out for air. I wondered audibly concerning the name of the place. An American companion looked at the signs round the station.

"It's Sortie," he said.

But it wasn't. It was Angoulême, and I wouldn't mind moving thither. My American friend was probably from Exit, Michigan.

The discovery was made and reported that one might go into the dining-car and smoke as much as one liked without asking permission from the maiden with the dreamy eyes. This car was filled with French soldiers and officers going back to the front after their holiday. There seemed to be as many different uniforms as there were men, and the scenery indoors was almost as brilliant as that out-side.

It was about eight-thirty in the evening when we reached Paris. The sophisticated soldiers engaged their "redcaps" before they left the train, calling to them through the open windows. The demand was much greater than the supply, and I was among the unfortunates who had to carry their own bag-gage. I staggered to a street where a whole flotilla of taxis was anchored, but when I asked for one the person in charge said "No, no, no, no, no," meaning "No," and pointed around the corner. I followed his directions and landed on a boulevard along which there was a steady procession of machines, but it was fully twenty minutes before one came that was going slow enough to stop.

Our city is not all lit up like a church these nights, and it was impossible to see much of what we passed on the way to the hotel.

At the desk an English clerk, dressed for a noon wedding, gave me a blank to fill out. All the blank wanted to know was my past family history. It is to be sent, said the clerk, to the prefect of police. I had no idea he was interested in me.

Sunday, August 19. Paris.

When I get back to Chicago I shall insist that
my favorite restaurant place tables out on the walk.
It is more hygienic and much more interesting.

But Chicago, I'm afraid, can't provide half as
much sidewalk entertainment as Paris. As I remember the metropolis of Illinois, there is a sad
lack there of demonstrative affection on the streets.
In fact, I fear that a lady and gentleman who kissed
each other repeatedly at the corner of Madison and
Dearborn would be given a free ride to Central
Station and a few days in which to cool off. Such
an osculatory duel on Paris's Grand Boulevard—
also known by a dozen other names—goes practically unnoticed except by us Illinois hicks.

An American officer and I—at the former's expense—lunched sur curb to-day. The food was
nothing to boast about, but we got an eyeful of
scenery. Soldiers—French, British and American
—strolled by constantly, accompanied by more or
less beautiful brunettes, and only a few were
thoughtless enough not to stop and kiss a few times

Only a few were thoughtless enough not to stop and kiss a few
times in full view of our table

in full view of our table.   We also observed the inmates of passing taxis.   No matter how wide the
back seat, the lady occupant invariably sat on her
escort's lap.   A five-passenger car in America is a
ten-passenger car in Paris, provided the chauffeur
has a girl of his own.

When the American officer was tired of buying,
I left him and sought out the *Chicago Tribune*
office, conveniently located above Maxim's.   The
editor was there, but he was also broke, so I went
back to the Ritz and got ready for bed.

The express office will be open to-morrow and I
will be a rich man.

Lundi, 20 Août.   Paris.

Went down to the express office and cashed a
large part of my order.   Friends were with me, and
they immediately relieved me of most of the burden.
I was hungry for lunch, having had no breakfast.
Meat was what I wanted, and meat was what I
couldn't get.   Which led me to inquire into the
Rules de la vie of Paris.

1.   Monday and Tuesday are meatless days.

2.   All except Saturday and Sunday are heatless days.   Hot baths are impossible on Mondays, Tuesdays, Wednesdays, Thursdays and Fridays.

3.   Strong liquor is procurable between noon and two P. M. and seven-thirty and nine-thirty at night. At other times ye toper must be content with light wines.

4.   All public places except the theaters must close and douse lights at nine-thirty in the evening.

5.   There is no speed limit for taxis or privately owned cars.   A pedestrian run over and killed is liable to imprisonment.   The driver is not only innocent, but free to hurl as many French curses as he likes at his victims.   If the pedestrian is not killed, he must explain why not to the judge.

6.   It is not only permissible but compulsory to speak to any girl who speaks to you, and a girl who won't speak to you should be reported to the police.

7.   No watch or clock is wrong.   Whatever time you have is right and you may act accordingly.

8.   Matches never ignite.   A smoker must purchase a cigar or cigarette lighter and keep it filled

with essence, the française term for gas. Sometimes the lighters work.

9. American cigarettes are not procurable. Bum ones may be bought at any tabac store or café for only five times what they are worth.

10. Water must never be used as a thirst quencher, and seldom for any other purpose. It's worse than bourgeois; it's unheard-of.

The lack of water, hot or cold, drove me to a barber shop this morning. The barber first made me put on a shroud, and I was afraid he was either going to cut me to pieces or talk me to death. But his operation was absolutely painless and his incessant conversation harmless, because I couldn't understand a word of it.

From the barber shop I went to the information department of American Army Headquarters. That's where you get permits to visit our camps. But of course, if you've run over here from America, you have lots of spare time on your hands, so they're doing you a favor if they hold you up a few days. What is a week or so when a man's here for a whole month?

They have queer ideas at the Maison de la Presse, which is the French equivalent for our publicity bureau. They receive you cordially there and treat you just as if you were not dregs.

I jumped thither after a futile visit to our own headquarters. I said I would like to go to the French front.

"Certainly," replied the man in charge. "Whenever is convenient for you, we'll see that you get a trip."

So I told him when it would be convenient and he's going to see me through. I hear that the British are similarly peculiar. They are polite even to newspaper men and magazine writers. They might even speak to a cartoonist.

Returning to our side of the Seine, I bumped into some Australians, here on leave. One had been in Germany before the war and could speak and understand the "schoenste language."

"They use me as an interpreter," he said. "When they bring in a bloody boche prisoner, I talk to him. First we give him a real meal, maybe bacon and eggs and coffee, something he hasn't seen for

months.   Then I ask him where he came from and
how he got here.   Most of them are glad to tell
me the truth.   Those that do, I mark them down
as 'Very intelligent.'   Those that volunteer information I record as 'Extremely intelligent.'   Those
that say 'Nicht verstehe' go down in the record as
'Not intelligent.'   But the majority are so bloody
well glad to be out of the war that they talk freely.

"I asked one Heinie if he was going to try to
escape.   'Not me,' he said, 'I'm tickled to be here.'
They're all fed up on the war.   You'd be too with
three years of it."

This young man admitted that he was one of the
best football players in Australia.   "Maybe I've
forgotten how now," he said.   "I've been over here
three years.   Just think of it—I traveled twelve
thousand miles, or maybe it's kilos, to mix up in
this."

Baseball, he told me, had taken a strong hold on
Australia.

"I don't hit well," he said, "but I can catch what
you call flies!   I can catch the widest flies that are
knocked."

Which gift would probably be useless in America, where most of the flies knocked are bloody narrow.

Before I left him I learned also that Les Darcy was all right at heart, but that the professional "sports" spoiled him, and that he could have "knocked Jack Johnson, Stanley Ketchel, Billy Papke or Jess Willard clean out of the ring."

He is going back to the trenches to-night, and I hope there are plenty of extremely intelligent Heinies there to keep him busy interpreting till his next leave. Interpreting, I should think, would be much pleasanter than going over the top.

Tuesday, August 21.

This time it was an American of the French Ambulance Service.

"Say, listen," he said. "I can give you some mighty good stories. Real stuff, do you get me? Listen: One night there was a boche wounded out there and I brought him in. He had one leg all shot to pieces and we had to operate. I was going to give him the ether when he turned over and looked me in the face. 'Why, Dan,' he said, 'aren't

you going to speak to me?' It was a chap I'd gone
to school with in America. I could give you lots
of stuff like that; do you get me? I used to be in
New York, and Rube Goldberg used to call me up
out of bed at six in the morning. 'Dan,' he'd say
to me, 'I'm up against it for an idea. Will you give
me an idea?' Do you get me? And there's a
dramatic critic in New York—I won't tell you his
name—but he used to tag around me after a first
night and ask me what I thought of the show. Do
you get me? I can give you a lot of good stuff."

I told him I was afraid that if he gave it to me
all at once I wouldn't remember any of it. So he
is coming to my hotel every day during his leave,
to give me a little at a time—if he can find me.

Last night a good-hearted American officer took
me to dinner at La Tour d'Argent, which is said
to be the oldest restaurant in Paris and which, they
say, is the place the Kaiser was going to have his
banquet on a certain night three years ago if Gott
hadn't gone back on him at the last moment.

We ordered duck, the restaurant's specialty.
They cook it in your presence, slice off whatever is

sliceable, and then put the bird in a press and give you the result as gravy. After the meal they hand you a post card on which is inscribed *le numéro de votre canard.* I looked up "canard" in my dictionary and found that it meant a drake, or false news, or a worthless newspaper. I have heard lots of false news, but I know no one took the trouble to count the items. Also I know that my newspaper is neither worthless nor numbered. So canard in this case must mean drake. The number of mine was 41654. If he had happened to disagree with me, I could have taken his number and traced him to the source. It's a very good idea and might be used in America on eggs or drinks.

I made another trip to the office which is supposed to be in charge of American correspondents and accommodations for them. I will go there again to-morrow and again the next day. I will bother them to death. Meantime I have applied to a person in London for permission to go to the British front, and have been assured a visit to the French lines late next week. I have wonderful vision and can see things twelve miles away.

P. S.   It was revealed to me to-night that my detention and trial in Bordeaux was a frame-up conceived by loving friends aboard ship and carried out by that English-speaking cross-examiner, who, believe me, is a convincing actor.

Thanks, gents. It was good for about two thousand words.

III

I TRY TO GET TO THE AMERICAN CAMP —BUT MEET DISASTER

Wednesday, August 22.   Paris.

The gentlemen authorized to issue visitors' passes to the American camp and the various fronts don't seem to realize that a person may be in a hurry. They fail to appreciate the facts that hanging round Paris is financial ruin and that the world series, which one positively must attend, is drawing nearer every hour.

Permission to go to the British front was requested over a week ago.   No reply.   Daily calls at our own press bureau produce nothing but promises of a trip somewhere, some time.   Monsieur Boss of the French Maison de la Presse says I may be taken through the devastated territory—in a week or so.

Meanwhile the Battle of Paris goes on, with Death always staring one in the face—Death from taxis, from starvation, from water thirst, from hand-to-hand encounters with the language.

Death from a taxi is the most likely form and the most distressing, for under the Parisian law the person run down and killed is the one at fault and the corpus delicti is liable to life imprisonment or worse. A pedestrian has no more rights here than the Kaiser, and it's almost impossible to cross the street unless you've gone through a course of intensive training in Detroit.

There would be little danger if all the crossings were on the upgrade, for the French cars—those which aren't in the military service—have a desperate time climbing. They have to shift speeds even to run up on the sidewalk, which is one of their favorite sports. But the Loop District of Paris is topographically on the level, and taxis can tear along like an eastbound Russian.

On occasions when you are run into and knocked down a gendarme appears on the scene with pencil and note-book. He takes the name and address of the driver and escorts you to jail. If you die there, the driver is sent a medal for marksmanship.

Taxi fares are cheaper, probably, than anywhere else in the world. They amount to practically nothing if you have an accident—that is, a trip without a collision with something or somebody. But even if you enjoy an average tour and hit a building or another vehicle or a dog or a person, they soak you only about half as much as they would in New York or Chicago, where there are far fewer thrills per drive.

The tariff from the hotel where I put up (I haven't found out how much) to American General Headquarters, where I go every morning to be refused a pass to the camps, is one franc cinquante if you miss all targets. This forenoon it was two francs cinquante because we knocked the rear wheel off a young boy's bicycle.

The boy, after a hearty bawling out by the driver and two gendarmes, was carted to a police station. They'll hardly keep him in jail, though. Matteawan is the proper place for a boy who attempts bicycling on the streets of Paris.

W. MORGAN

A pedestrian has no more rights here than the Kaiser, and it's
almost impossible to cross the street unless you've gone
through a course of intensive training in Detroit

Thursday, August 23.   Paris.

One of several differences between an American and a Frenchman is that an American tries to understand a Frenchman's English and a Frenchman tries not to understand an American's French.

To-day I wanted to go from somewhere to the Hotel Continental.

"Hotel Con-tin-ent-al," I said to the driver.

He shook his head. I repeated. He shook his head again. This went on till I had pronounced the name five times and he had shaken his head that often. I said it the sixth time just as I had said it the other five.

"Oh-h-h!" shouted the driver, his face lighting up. "Hotel Con-tin-ent-al!"

And there wasn't a particle of difference between his version and mine.

There was excitement in our village last night. At twenty-three-thirty o'clock, as we Parisians say, began a chorus of screaming sirens, the warning signal of an air raid. Those of us living in up-stairs rooms experienced a sudden craving for a

home Somewhere in the Basement, and in gratify-
ing it didn't stop to use the elevator. The majority taking part in the Great Descent wore pa-
jamas or their female relatives, sometimes called
chemises de nuit. A few, of which I was one, were
still attired for the day, and we went outdoors and
looked up.

A regular flock of planes was, you might say,
planely visible, but there was no fight in the air
and no dropping of bombs on our fair city. The
birdmen soared round a while in a perfectly friendly
manner and then retired to their nests. The sirens
were stilled and we all went up-stairs, the majority,
mentioned above, grateful for the war-time lack of
lights.

It seems that a Frenchman, returning from his
day's toil, forgot to flash his password, which is a
red tail-light, or something. And the patrol took
him for a boche and gave chase. Fortunately for
himself, he glimpsed his pursuers in time and
turned on the required signal.

To-day there has been a big demand for first-
floor rooms.

Friday, August 24.   Paris.

An American major—it is interdict by the censor to mention the names of any officers save General Sibert and General Pershing—asked a friend in London to buy him an automobile and ship it here for his use. The Londoner was able, after much difficulty, to purchase one of those things that grow so rapidly in Detroit. He packed it up and mailed it to Le Havre. From there it had to be driven to Paris.

The major had never learned to drive this particular brand. In fact, his proportions are such that not even a shoehorn could coax him into the helmsman's seat. He asked me to go up and get it for him. I declined on grounds of neutrality. That was a week ago.

Well, yesterday one Mr. Kiley, who has been over here some time in the ambulance service, came back to town with the car and four flat tires, which, evidently, were far past the draft age when the sale was made in London. Mr. Kiley helped himself to a stimulant and then told me about his trip.

He reached Le Havre last Saturday afternoon. He had in his pockets no papers except an order for the car. He had been in Le Havre about two minutes when a gentleman attacked him from behind with a tap on the shoulder. The gentleman pulled back his coat lapel and flashed a star bearing the insignia of the British Intelligence Department. He was curious as to Mr. Kiley's name and business. Mr. Kiley told him. Then he wanted to see Mr. Kiley's papers. Mr. Kiley showed him the order for the car.

"I'm afraid that won't do," said the officer. "I'd advise you to leave town."

"Give me just an hour," pleaded Mr. Kiley, "just time enough to get the car and get out."

"All right," said the officer, "and be sure it's only an hour."

Mr. Kiley hastened to where the car was reposing, displayed the order, and started joyously to wind her up. He cranked and he cranked and he cranked. Nothing doing. He gave her a push downhill and tried to throw her into speed. Nothing doing. It occurred to him that something must be the matter. A thorough examination resulted in a correct diagnosis. There was no gas.

Next to getting a drink of ice-water in Paris, the hardest job for a stranger is buying gasoline in any French town. Mr. Kiley was turned down five times before eighteen o'clock, when all the garages closed for the day.

He registered at a hotel and went into the café for dinner. He was just picking up the carte du jour when his friend, the officer, horned in.

"Mr. Kiley," says this guy, "you have been in town more than an hour."

"Yes, sir," said Mr. Kiley. "But I've had trouble. I found my car, but I can't run it because there's no essence."

"I think you'd better leave town," said the officer.

"If you don't mind," said Mr. Kiley, "I'll leave early in the morning."

"I wouldn't mind if you left right now," said he.

There followed a long discussion and a cross-examination even crosser than mine in Bordeaux. Mr. Kiley revealed his whole family history and won the right to stay overnight, provided he remained indoors and departed from town first thing in the morning.

But France is like America in that Saturday is usually succeeded by Sunday, and when Mr. Kiley arose from his hotel bed and resumed his search for gas he found every garage in town shut up tight. As I remember the United States, garages do not keep holy the Sabbath Day nor any other day. Over here, however, everything closes on Sunday except churches, theaters and saloons.

Mr. Kiley took in the situation and returned to his room to hide. Shortly before midi there was a knock at his door and a new officer appeared.

"You seem to like our town, Mr. Kiley," said he.

"I'll leave it as soon as I can get away," said Mr. Kiley.

"No doubt," replied the officer. "But I believe you will be here a long while."

Mr. Kiley tried to look calm.

"Bone," he said in perfectly good French.

"For the present," said the officer, "you must not leave the hotel. Later on we'll talk things over."

In the café on Sunday night Mr. Kiley met an

American and told him his troubles. The American had a car of his own in Le Havre and plenty of gasoline. He would be glad to give Mr. Kiley enough to start him on his way.

"But I can't go," said Mr. Kiley, "till I've fixed it with the police. I'll have to look for them."

He didn't have far to look. No. 2 was in the lobby.

"Yes," said No. 2, "you can leave town if you leave quick. There must be no more foolishness. The only thing that saves you from arrest is your uniform."

Mr. Kiley left town and left quick, and, aside from his four blow-outs, had an uneventful trip to Paris.

But what if I had taken that assignment—I with no uniform except one willed me by the Chicago Cubs? O Boy!

Saturday, August 25.   Paris.

On advice of counsel I went to Colonel Anonymous of the American General Staff and besought him to fix it so that I might get to one of our camps without further stalling.   Colonel Anonymous said it was all right with him and telephoned to Major Noname, who seemed to have authority in affaires journalistic.

Major Noname, fortunately, is a baseball fan. I told him what I did know, and lots that I didn't know about our national pastime, and the reward was an American press pass to the infantry camp, S. in F.

I am going in a horseless carriage with Joe and Howard, fellow conspirators in the so-called journalistic game, and the start is to be made early Monday morning.   Joe is going to drive his own car, and I hope he knows how.

Dimanche, 26 Août. Paris.

Yesterday was Saturday, and everybody had had a hot bath and felt like doing something.   Three of us decided to take in the highly recommended show at Les Ambassadeurs.

A member of the Theatrical Geographic Society met us in the foyer and showed us a map of the playhouse.   From it we were supposed to pick our seats. We chose three that, on paper, were in the sixth row in the center aisle. Our usher, female, led us to three which were in the tenth row, off to one side. Our usher stuck round as if she expected something. I was the party with the seat checks, and she got nothing. I was ignorant of the rules of the game. But not for long. Pretty soon in came three of the World's Greatest Fighters, alias Canadian soldiers, and sat down behind us. Their usher was more persistent than mine.

"What do you want?" demanded one who seemed to be the financial leader. "I already gave you a franc."

"Un franc pour trois?" said the lady in horror.

"Yes, and that's enough," said the Canuck. "Aller!" he added in perfect Canadian.

"Je ne comprend pas," said the lady.

"Go to the devil then!" said the Canadian in perfect Portuguese.

The lady went somewhere, but whether to the proper destination I do not know.

"I wonder how much they charge to get out," wondered the Canadian.

Along about the middle of the show our own usher popped up before me and held out her right hand, at the same time exhibiting both teeth in an ingratiating smile. I shook the proffered hand. She withdrew her teeth.

"Non, non, non, non," she said.

I asked her what she voulez-voued. She was coy.

"Do you want a tip?" I inquired in plain Michigan.

Both teeth reappeared. A dental curiosity drove me to hand her three francs. I had not underestimated.

In the second act a very nice-looking lady sang *A Broken Doll* in plain Thirty-ninth Street. The stage chorus tried to help her out on the second refrain, but, with all due modesty, I must say that it was the Canadians and I who earned the vociferous encore.

Lundi, 27 Août. Paris.

The first batch of laundry was back when I returned from the theater Saturday night. Collars were done up in a neat package, tied with baby-blue ribbon. They looked just as when I had sent them out except that there was a high, shiny polish over the soiled spots. As for handkerchiefs, let us follow the British communiqué style:

"Eleven of our handkerchiefs went over the Blanchisserie lines. Two came back. Nine are missing."

Some practical joker suggested that I go out yesterday afternoon and watch a baseball game between a Canadian team and a club from the American Red Cross. St. Cloud was the battle ground. You pronounce St. Cloud exactly as it is not spelled.

A taxi man took us out there by way of Kansas City and El Paso, and during the forty minutes' trip he was in high speed at least one minute. We bumped into a ceremony of awards. French soldiers to the number of two hundred were being given the Croix de Guerre.

The ceremony over, we crossed the race track and got on to the baseball field. There was an hour of badly needed practise, and then the two belligerents went at each other in a so-called ball game. It was stopped at the end of the eighth inning on account of rain, eight innings too late.

The rain, I am told, was long overdue, and we may expect gobs of it between now and then.

I am writing this early Monday morning, and early Monday morning is when we were supposed to start for the American camp. But there seems to be a difference of opinion over the meaning of the French adverb "early."

Tuesday, August 28. Somewhere in France.

"Early" proved to be half past ten yesterday morning. Joe drove us to the city limits, and there we had to pause. According to this year's rules, ye automobilist pauses at the limits, has his gasoline measured, and then goes on. Returning to town, he has to pay a tax on the added amount of gasoline he brings, or something like that.

We were allowed to go out of town, and some thirty yards beyond the limits we found a garage. There we filled up with essence. Howard did the cranking, which is a necessity with all French cars, and away we went.

It was raining and it was cold. Joe and Howard were in the front seat, Joe driving and Howard studying the road map. I was in the back seat, catching cold.

"We'll go right ahead," said Joe, "to Such and Such a Place, and there we'll stop and have lunch."

Well, we stopped in Such and Such a Place, but it was not from a desire of lunch. It was because we were compelled to stop.

"Let's see your papers," said the stopper in French.

The stoppees, in English, displayed their passes to the American camp. The stopper didn't know whether they were good or not. He asked us to wait a moment and disappeared out of the rain. We waited several moments. Finally there appeared another stopper, who read carefully our passes and told us they were no good and that we would have to loom up at the City Hall.

We went there, with Joe and Howard in the front seat and an officer and I in the back, me still catching cold, especially in the feet.

In the City Hall were French officers attired in

all colors of the French army, which made the colors of the rainbow look like Simon Pure White. Our crime, it seems, was in not having an automobile pass on a red card. Or maybe it was blue. One of the thirty gentlemen in charge said we would have to wait till he telephoned back to Paris. Knowing the French telephone system, we inquired whether we might go across the street and eat. We were told we might.

We went across the street and ate, and it was a good meal, with meat, on a day which was meatless in Paris. A subaltern interrupted the orgy and said we were wanted back in the City Hall. Back there the startling information was that no telephonic satisfaction had been obtained. We asked whether we might go back to the café. There was no objection. We played pitch. French soldiers by scores came up and looked on. Joe thought, sub rosa, that it would be a grand idea to startle 'em. So we played pitch for one hundred francs a hand, it being tacitly understood that the money didn't go. But we certainly had them excited.

Between pitch games in which thousands of

francs were apparently lost and won, we visited, on summons, the City Hall five or six times. Every time there was the same heavy barrage of français.

Entered, finally, an English-speaking gent who said we might leave the city provided we went straight back to Paris.

"We'd much prefer," said Joe, "to go on to where we were going."

"You have the choice," was the reply, "of returning to Paris or remaining here, in jail."

Paris sounded the more attractive. They gave us back our car and away we went. It was after twenty o'clock, and it was pitch dark, and it was cold, and it was raining. And the man who had made the machine had forgotten to equip it with headlights.

A little before midnight, on the downhill main street of a village, we saw ahead of us a wagon. It was two feet ahead of us. There being nothing else to do we banged into it. Then we stopped. The driver of the wagon sat suddenly down in the middle of the street and apologized. We all got out to see whether any damage had been done to the car. The only wounds discernible in the darkness were a smashed radiator and a bent axle.

"It's lucky this happened in a town," said I. "We can probably find a hotel."

"We're not going to look for one," said Joe. "We're going to drive to Paris."

We got back in and, to our amazement, the darn thing started. There was plenty of headlight now, for the whole hood was ablaze. All lit up like a church, we went on our mad career until our convey-ance dropped dead, overcome by the heat. This was four miles from a town that will be famous in the histories of this war.

"I guess we're through," said Joe. "One of us will have to stay with the car and see that nothing is stolen. The other two can go back to town and find a bed."

By a vote of two to one, Howard was elected to stay with the car. He was the youngest.

Joe and I hiked our four miles in silence. The town was as brilliantly lighted as a cemetery and apparently void of inmates. We groped for an hour in a vain search for a hostelry. At length we gave up and resolved to sleep on the huge cathedral's front porch. We were ascending the steps when a door opened and a human being stood before us.

"Arrested again," thought I.

But the human being turned out to be not a copper, but a priest.

"Bon soir, monsieur," said Joe. "Voulez-vous show us où we can find a hotel?"

He led us across the street to a place we had doped out as the high school. He rapped on the door with his foot. In a few moments an aged lady, dressed for the night, appeared. There was a rapid exchange of français, after which we thanked the priest and were taken through a courtyard and up-stairs to our room. We said a prayer for Howard and went to sleep, and I had a nightmare. I dreamed of a porterhouse steak.

This morning we decided it wouldn't be clubby to have breakfast before we had rescued Howard and the car. We went to a garage which was equipped with a beautiful lady, but no automobiles nor tow-ropes. We found a livery stable that had every thing but a horse. We commandeered a young man's delivery cart from in front of a grocery store and drove out to the scene of our car's demise. Howard and the corpse were still there. Howard thought it would be a good idea to go to the near-est farm-house and rent a horse and a rope from the proprietor. The proprietor was very ignorant. He couldn't understand our French. But in his employ was a German prisoner who could talk his own language and ours and the funny one that is pre-valent round here. He explained our wants to the farmer and there ensued a few moments of hag-gling over price. We finally rented two horses and a rope for fifty francs and dragged the car back to town. From the looks of it, in daylight, I would say the economical course would have been to leave it out there in the road and keep the fifty francs.

The garage man says, in English, that he can make the necessary "reparations" in three weeks. So far as I'm concerned, he can devote three years to the job. Hereafter I'll do my cross-country flitting about on a train.

It's on one now, Paris bound, that I'm writing.

There is nothing to do but write, for Howard is getting the sleep he missed last night and Joe is too angry to talk.   He has spoken one sentence since we got up this morning.

"This is a queer war," he said.

IV

FINALLY I GET TO THE AMERICAN CAMP; WHAT I FIND THERE

Thursday, August 30. At an American Camp.

ME and a regular American correspondent, Mr. Bazin, who has been here since before the war, but is still good-natured, took the train from Paris this morning and reached our destination shortly after lunch time. This is one of a string of villages in which the main body of the Expeditionary Forces are billeted.

We were met at the train by one of the correspondents' cars, a regular he-man of a car from home, with eight cylinders and everything. Each correspondent rents a seat in one of the machines at a cost of sixty dollars a week. For this trifling sum he may be driven anywhere he wants to go along the line.

The correspondents have a tough life. They are

quartered in a good—judged by French star dards —hotel, and are not what you could call overworked. There is nothing to write about, and if you wrote about it you probably couldn't get it through.

Mr. Corey, one of these slaves, invited me to accompany him to an infantry billet, some eighteen miles distant. We sailed along over the perfect roads at an average speed of about sixty, slowing up in the villages to dodge a harmless course among the cows, chickens and children, all of whom use the middle of Main Street for their playground.

We passed an occasional soldier, but it was a nice clear day, and the large majority were out in the fields and hills rehearsing. Our boys, I'm told, are getting quite a workout. Usually they leave their billets at seven in the morning, walk from six to twelve miles to a drill ground, and work till half past four in the afternoon. Then they take the long hike "home" and wonder how soon supper will be ready. Frequently, however, there is practise in night trench warfare, and then the grind continues till ten or eleven o'clock. The work is hard, but so, by this time, are the boys.

The captain on whom we called said he was glad to meet me, which is the first time that has happened in France. We asked him whether there was any news. He said yes, that the Salvation Army had established headquarters in the camp.

"I'm glad," he remarked, "that they've decided to go in on our side. It may influence the Kaiser's friend Gott."

The chief need of the soldiers, he went on, was amusement. The Salvation Army's and Y. M. C. A.'s efforts were appreciated, but continual rations of soup and meat palled at times, and a little salad and dessert, in the form of Charlie Chaplin or the Follies, would make life more bearable.

"Some American theatrical producer," said the captain, "could win our undying gratitude by shipping over a stock company with a small repertory of shows, with music, and *girls*. I believe he'd find it profitable too. When the boys get paid they don't know what to do with their money. There's nothing to spend it on in these parts."

The captain invited us to dinner, but we had a previous date with members of the Censorship

Bureau. These entertained us with stories which I voluntarily delete. From their hotel we returned to our own, held a brief song service in the correspondents' mess, and called it a day.

Friday, August 31.   At an American Camp.

"Would you like to meet General Sibert?" asked Mr. Corey.

General Sibert's name is one of the two that may be mentioned.

I said I would, and we left after breakfast for the next village, where headquarters is situate. In the outer office were some clerks and a colonel. The latter could never be accused of excessive cordiality.

"The general is busy," he said.

"How long will he be busy?" inquired Mr. Corey.

"I have no idea," said the colonel.

Mr. Corey and I felt we would be warmer outdoors, so we climbed back in our car and asked our sergeant-driver to take us to the nearest training grounds. Here an infantry regiment was going through simple drill, and calisthentics which were far from simple.

The nearest captain approached, smiled pleasantly and asked what he could do for us. We introduced ourselves.

"Correspondents, eh?" he said.

"Well, then, you can do something for us—make the newspapers and magazines quit calling us Sammies. We've never done anything to deserve a name like that."

"What's the matter with it?" we inquired.

"Everything!" said the captain. "It doesn't fit, it sounds childish, and we just naturally hate it."

We asked him whether there was an acceptable substitute.

"I don't know of any," he said. "In due time we'll wish one on ourselves that will have pep and sound real. Meanwhile call us Julias, Howards—anything you like, except Sammies."

We promised to do our best for him, and he was grateful enough to invite us to his mess for lunch.

This young man—he looks about twenty-nine—hasn't been to his home, somewhere out West, since he left West Point, six years ago. He hasn't seen a show in six years. Mexico and the Philippines have kept him busy. His promotion from lieutenant to captain is very recent, and he still wears only one stripe. "I suppose I'll be a major before I get the other," he said. "A man can hardly keep up with his rank these days."

He called our attention to the physical condition of his men.

"You've got to be in the pink to go through those exercises without yelling for help," he said. "These fellas couldn't have done it a month ago. Now they seldom get tired, though the hours are pretty stiff. To-day is a cinch. It's pay-day, and there's a muster soon after lunch. So most of us will get a half holiday and nobody'll object."

The captain blew his whistle to indicate that the game was over. His boys quit happily, and we left him after agreeing to show up at his billet in time for lunch.

"We have a fairly good cook," he promised. "But what is much more important, we have a beautiful young lady to wait on us."

Our next stop was at a trench school. Americans,

under French tutelage, had constructed a perfect
—so we were told—system of ditches and entanglements, and had shown aptitude in learning the offensive and defensive points of this pleasant method
of warfare. They were now engaged in bomb-
throwing drill. Some of them had tried the baseball throw, but had found the grenades too heavy.
Several crooked-arm throws would do things to a
person's elbow. But, according to the officers, the
youngsters had done very well with the bowling
motion and had surprised the French with their
accuracy.

This officer, another captain, spoke in compli-
mentary terms of the French assistance.

"They've been more than diligent with us," said
he. "They've never shown impatience when we
failed to grab their point, but have gone over it
and over it till we've learned it to suit them. The
difference in languages makes it hard sometimes
to get what they're after, but they eventually manage to make themselves understood. The only fault
I have to find with them," he confided, "is that they

don't give us credit for knowing anything at all. They tell us this thing's a rifle, and the thing on the end of it is a bayonet, and so forth. And one of them showed me a barbed-wire entanglement one day, and told me what it was for. I'd always been under the mistaken impression that it was used for bed-clothes."

We had to turn down this captain's luncheon invitation, but we stopped at his house for light refreshment. His lieutenant, a young University of Michigan boy, had come over on the first transport, and related interesting details of that historic trip.

We went on to the other captain's, and lunched with him and his major and colonel. The beautiful young lady proved every bit as pretty as a pair of army shoes. But the food was good and the captain's French better. He kept hurling it at the beautiful young lady, who received it with derisive laughter. His accent, it appeared, was imposseeb.

"I like to make her laugh," he told me. "It takes me back home among the coyotes."

On the street of the village I held converse with a private, aged about twenty-three. I said I supposed he was glad it was pay-day.

"What's the difference!" he said. "I got more money now than Rockefella. I ain't spent more'n a buck since we been over, and then it was just to be spendin' it, not because they was anything to buy. I seen a fella the other day light a cigarette with one o' these here dirty twenty-franc notes. He was sick o' carrying it round. And they was another fella went up to one o' these here village belles and slipped her a hundred francs. He never seen her before, and he won't never see her again. He just says 'Souvenir' and let it go at that."

"Did she take it?"

"Oh, I guess not! She's to gay Paree by this time already."

"She won't burn up that town with a hundred francs."

"No, but all these girls don't think o' nothin' but gettin' there. From what I seen of it, I'd just as soon be in Akron."

"Oh, I'd hardly say that!"

"Talk about spendin' money! They was a poor fella here last week that got rid of a lot of it. He bought himself a bottle o' champagne wine. I don't think he'd tasted it before, but it's cheap over here. So he got a hold o' this bottle and poured it into him like it was excelsior water, and it acted on him like it was laughin' gas. He went up alongside the officers' billet and sang 'em a vocal solo. The captain heard him—you could of heard him in San Francisco—and the captain come out and invited him in. And when he got him in there he says: 'So-and-So, how much did this little bun cost you?' So the fella told him a buck and a half. So the captain says: 'You've underestimated the amount by about seventy bucks. You'll get your next pay the last day of October.' "

I asked my new friend how he liked his billet.

"Great!" he said. "I and a couple other fellas has a room next to a pig on one side and a flock o' chickens on the other. We never get lonesome, and it makes it nice and handy when we want some ham and eggs. I know one fella that rooms next to a settlement o' rats. Night times he sets his flashlight so's it throws a narrow path o' light acrost the floor, then he puts a little piece o' meat in the path and stands over it with a bayonet. When Mr. Rat gets there the fella comes down whang with the bayonet and fastens him to the floor. It's good target practise, and he'd ought to be sure fire by the time it's Huns instead o' rats."

"Maybe," said I, "the Huns would know better than to come out in the light."

"They'd go anywheres for a piece o' meat," said the private.

He had to depart and report for muster. We took another road home, a road frequented by sheep and railroad crossings, both of which slow you up considerably.

In France the gates—strong iron ones—at grade crossings are kept closed except when some one wants to cross the tracks. The some one makes known his desire by tooting his horn or shouting, and the gatekeeper—usually an old lady with the pipe-smoking habit—comes out of her shack and opens the gates, expending anywhere from ten minutes to half an hour on the task. The salary attached to the position is the same as that of a French private: ten centimes a day, which is two cents in regular money. I presume the gatekeepers have a hot time in the old town on pay night.

As for the sheep, when you come up behind them you might as well resign yourself to staying behind them till they reach the village for which they are headed. They won't get out of the way of their own accord, and neither the dog nor the aged shepherd will make any effort to sidetrack them.

Having led them into the village, the shepherd proceeds to deliver them to their respective owners. He stops in front of a house, plays a certain tune on his horn, and the sheep or sheeps belonging to that house step out of ranks and sheepishly retire for the night, or perhaps sit up a while in the parlor and talk war with the family.

There must be a lot of intermarrying among the sheeps of one village. A great many of those in the flock we saw looked enough alike to be cousins or something.

Somebody suggested a poker game for this evening's entertainment, but I got all I wanted of that great sport coming across the bounding blue.

It has rained only an hour in two days, and the boys say we'll get it good to-morrow.

Saturday, September 1.   In an American Camp.

As exclusively predicted by everybody, it was pouring when we arose this morning, but rain doesn't keep you indoors in France. If it did, you would live indoors.

We splashed the thirty miles to the other end of the camp and inflicted ourselves on a major of marines. He seemed deliberately unfriendly at first, but it was only his manner. After five minutes of awkward monosyllabic dialogue he gave us the usual refreshments and took us out to see the town, the name of which should be Mud if it isn't.

"This is a grand climate," he said. "They must have had conscription to get people to live here."

He took us to the camp kitchen, of which he was evidently and justly proud. It was a model of convenience and cleanliness. He spoke to the cook.

"Are you very busy?" he asked.

"No, sir," was the reply.

"Then I'd shave if I were you," said the major.

"Daily shaving," he told us when we got outside, "ought to be compulsory in our army as it is in the British. When a man hasn't shaved he isn't at his best, physically, morally, or mentally. When he has he's got more confidence in himself; his morale is better. Shaving has a psychological effect, and I try to impress my men with the importance of it. They say it's a difficult operation here, but I guess if the Tommies can do it in the trenches, we can in these billets."

We remarked on the increasing popularity of mustaches among the men.

"I don't object to them," said the major. "Neither do I see any sense to them. To my mind they're in a class with monocles or an appendix. But so long as the men keep their cheeks and chins smooth, they're at liberty to wear as much of a misplaced eyebrow as they can coax out."

The major showed us his hospital and his dentist shop and marched us up a steep hill, where, in the rain, we saw a great many interesting things and promised not to write about them.

After lunch we decided it would be patriotic to go home and remove our wet clothes. In my case, this meant spending the rest of the day in my room, and that's where I am.

Sunday, September 2. Paris.

The driver assigned to take me to the train, which left from the next village this morning, lost his way, and we reached the station just as the engine was sounding the Galli-Curci note that means All Aboard. There was no time to buy a ticket, and you can't pay a cash fare on a train in France. But the conductor, or whatever you call him here, said I could get a ticket at the destination, Paris; in fact, I must get a ticket or spend the rest of my unnatural life wandering about the station.

I found a seat in a compartment in which were a young American officer, beginning his forty-eight hours' leave, and a young French lady who looked as if she had been in Paris before. The young officer and I broke into conversation at once. The young lady didn't join in till we had gone nearly twenty kilomet's.

Captain Jones, which isn't his name, called attention to the signs on the window warning MM. Les Voyageurs to keep their anatomies indoors. The signs were in three languages. "Ne pas Pencher au Dehors," said the French. The English was "Danger to Lean Outside." And the Wop: "Non Sporgere"—very brief. It was evident that a fourth variation of the warning had been torn off, and it didn't require a William Burns to figure out in what language it had been written.

"If there were a boche on this train," said Captain Jones, "he could lean his head off without hurting any one's feelings."

"Languages are funny," continued the captain sagely. "The French usually need more words than we do to express the same thought. I believe that explains why they talk so fast—they've got so much more to say."

I inquired whether he knew French.

"Oh, yes," he said. "I've been over here so long that I can even tell the money apart."

The dining-car conductor came in to ask whether we wanted the first or second "série" luncheon. You must reserve your seat at table on trains here or you can't eat. We decided on the second, and so did our charming compartment mate. Captain Jones, supposing she could not understand English, said: "Shall you take her to lunch or shall I?"

I was about to be magnanimous when she remarked, with a scornful glance at the captain: "I shall myself take me to lunch if monsieur has no objection."

The cap was temporarily groggy, but showed wonderful recuperative powers and in five minutes convinced her that he would toss himself into the Seine if she refused to eat with us. She accepted, after some stalling that convinced me she had been cordially inclined all the while.

General polite conversation ensued, and soon came the inevitable French question: How many American soldiers were there in France? I have heard it asked a million times, and I have heard a million different answers. The captain gave the truthful reply: "I don't know."

"I shall myself take me to lunch if monsieur has no objections"

"This war," he said, "should be called the War
of Rumors.   The war will be over by Christmas.
The war won't be over for ten years.   The boche
is starving.   The Allies are getting fat.   The
boche has plenty to eat.   The Allies are dying of
hunger.   Our last transport fleet sank five subs.
Our last transport fleet was sunk by a whole flotilla
of subs.   Montenegro's going to make a separate
peace with Bosnia.   There is talk of peace negotia-
tions between Hungary and Indiana.   Ireland, Bra-
zil and Oklahoma are going to challenge the world.
They're going to move the entire war to the Bal-
kans and charge admission.   The Kaiser's dying of
whooping cough.   You can learn anything you want
to or don't want to know.   Why"—this to me—
"don't you fellas print the truth?"

"And where," I asked him, "would you advise
us to go and get it?"

"The same place I got it," said the captain.

"And what is it?"

"I don't know."

We adjourned to the diner.   A sign there said:
"Non Fumeurs."   The captain pointed to it.

"That's brief enough," he said. "That's once when the French is concise. But you ought to see the Chinese for that. I was in a town near the British front recently where some Chinese laborers are encamped. In the station waiting-room, it says: 'No Smoking' in French, English, Russian and Italian. The Russian is something like 'Do notski smokevitch,' and the Italian is 'Non Smokore'. Recently they have added a Chinese version, and it's longer than the Bible. A moderate smoker could disobey the rules forty times before he got through the first chapter and found out what they were driving at."

Be that as it may, I have observed that everybody in France smokes whenever and wherever he or she desires, regardless of signs. We did now, and so did our guest, while waiting for the first course, which was black bread baked in a brickyard.

"I would love to go to America," said mademoiselle.

"You wouldn't care for it," replied the captain promptly. "It's too wild."

"How is it wild?"

"Every way: manners, habits, morals. The majority of the people, of course, are Indians, and you just can't make them behave."

She asked whether either of us had ever been in New York. The captain said he'd passed through there once on the way to Coney Island. She wanted to know if New York was bigger than Paris. "It's bigger than France," said Captain Jones.

Monsieur was trying to make a game of her.

"Well, anyway," said the captain, "you could lose France in Texas."

What was Texas?

"Texas," said the captain, "is the place they send soldiers when they've been bad. It's way out west, near Chicago."

The lady had heard of Chicago.

"This gentleman works there," said the captain. "He's part Indian, but he was educated at Carlisle and is somewhat civilized. He gets wild only on occasions."

The lady regarded me rather scaredly.

"He lives on the plains outside the city," continued the captain, "and rides to his work and back on a zebra. Practically all the suburban savages have zebras, and the Chicago traffic police have a fierce time handling them during their owners' working hours. They run wild around the streets and in the department stores, and snap at women, especially brunettes."

We had attained the potato course. The French positively will not serve potatoes as other than a separate course. I was about to help myself to a generous portion when the captain cried: "Here! Better leave those things alone. You know what they do to you."

I told him I didn't believe two or three would hurt, and proceeded to take three.

"When a half Indian eats potatoes," said the captain, "he usually forgets himself and runs amuck."

Our guest probably didn't know what a muck was, but it had an unpleasant sound, and the look she gave me was neither friendly nor trusting.

"The greatest difference between France and America," continued Captain Jones, "is in the people. In America a man ordinarily takes the initia-

tive in striking up an acquaintance with a woman.
He has to speak to her before she'll speak to him.
This would never do in France, where the men are
too shy. Then there's a difference in the way men
treat their wives and horses. Americans use whips
instead of clubs. And Americans have funny ideas
about their homes. Private bedrooms and play-
rooms are provided for their pets—zebras, lizards
and wild cats—and the little fellows are given to
understand that they must remain in them and not
run all over the house, like one of your cows."

He paused to ask me how the potatoes were acting. I said it was too soon to tell, but I felt a little
dizzy in the head. He suggested it were better to
go back to our compartment, where there were less
things to throw in the event of my reaching the
throwing stage.

"On the other hand," I said, "if I am deprived of
knives, forks and plates, I will pick on human be-
ings, and I usually aim out the windows."

But he said he was sick of the atmosphere in the
diner. We asked for l'addition and argued over who
should pay it. I won, and when he had been given

his change we returned to our own car, where mademoiselle demonstrated her fear of my expected outbreak by going to sleep.

We turned our attention to the scenery, the most striking feature of which was the abundance of boche prisoners at work in the fields.

"Lucky stiffs!" said the captain. "The war is over for them if they can just manage not to escape, and I guess there's no difficulty about that. Better food than the soldiers, a soft job, and a bed to sleep in. And wages besides. Every private in the Fritz army would surrender if the officers hadn't given them a lot of bunk about the way German prisoners are treated. They make them believe we cut off their feet and ears and give them one peanut and a glass of water every two weeks."

Paris hove into view, and we quarreled about the girl. The fair thing, we decided, would be to turn over her and her baggage to a porter and wish her many happy returns of the day. We were spared this painful duty, however, for when she awoke she treated both of us as strangers. And the gentleman who attended to her baggage was not a porter, but a French aviator, waiting on the station platform for that very purpose.

"She'll tell him," guessed the captain, "that an American soldier and half Indian tried to flirt with her on the train, but she froze them out."

Captain Jones stuck with me till my exit ticket was procured, a chore that ate up over an hour. Then we climbed into a dreadnought and came to this hotel, where I sat right down and versified as follows:

TO AN AMERICAN SOLDIER

If you don't like the nickname Sammy,
If it's not all a nickname should be,
You can pick out Pat or Mike,
Whatever name you like—
It won't make no difference to me.
Want a Thomas or Harry or Dick name?
Dost prefer to be called Joe or Lou?
You've a right to your choice of a nickname;
Oh, Mr. Yank, it's up to you.

V

MY ADVENTURES AT THE BRITISH FRONT

Monday, September 3. Paris.

IN this morning's mail was a letter from Somewhere in London, replying favorably to my request to go to the British front. I was directed to take the letter to the assistant provost marshal, who would slip me a pass and inform me as to the details of the trip.

At the A. P. M.'s I was given the pass and with it "an undertaking to be signed by all intending visitors to the front." There are ten rules in the undertaking, and some of them are going to be hard to obey. For example:

"I understand that it is impossible to arrange for me to see relatives serving with the fighting forces."

"I will not visit the enemy front during the present war."

But No. 6 is the tough one:

"In no circumstances will I deliver a political or electioneering speech to troops."

I must pray for strength to resist natural impulses along this line.

Wednesday morning, said the A. P. M., would be our starting time. And he told us when and where to take the train—"us" because I am to be accompanied by a regular correspondent, one who carries a cane and everything.

Mr. Gibbons, the regular correspondent, informs me I must wear a uniform, and to-morrow morning I am to try on his extra one, which he has kindly offered.

Another chore scheduled for to-morrow is the squaring of myself with the boss of the French Maison de la Presse, who invited me to visit the devastated territory Thursday and Friday. The invitation was accepted, but the British and French dates conflict, and I would rather see one real, live front than any number of broken-down barns and boched trees.

Tuesday, September 4. Paris.

I reported, after the French idea of breakfast, at the Maison de la Presse. This is situate on the fourth floor of a building equipped with an elevator that proves the fallacy of the proverb "What goes up must come down." You can dimly see it at the top of the shaft, and no amount of button pushing or rope pulling budges it.

During the long climb I rehearsed the speech of apology and condolence framed last night, and wondered whether monsieur would be game and try to smile or break down completely or fly into a rage. He was game, and he not only tried to smile, but succeeded. And his smile was in perfect simulation of relief. These French are wonderful actors.

I returned thence to Mr. Gibbons' room for my fitting. His extra uniform consisted of a British officer's coat and riding breeches, puttees and shoes. Cap and khaki shirt I had to go out and purchase. The store I first selected was a gyp joint and wanted twenty-seven francs for a cap. I went to another store and got exactly the same thing for twenty-six. A careful shopper can save a lot of money in Paris.

Provided with cap and shirt, the latter costing a franc less than the former, I went to a secluded spot and tried on the outfit, Mr. Gibbons assisting. We managed the puttees in thirty-five minutes. It is said that a man working alone can don them in an hour, provided he is experienced.

"You look," Mr. Gibbons remarked when I was fully dressed, "as if you had been poured into it."

But I felt as if I hadn't said "when" quite soon enough. Mr. Gibbons and I differ in two important particulars—knee joints—and though I tried to seem perfectly comfortable, my knees were fairly groaning to be free of the breeches and out in the open fields.

"Wear it the rest of the day and get used to it," advised Mr. Gibbons.

"No," I said. "I don't want to rumple it all up. I want to keep it neat for to-morrow." And against his protest I tore myself out and resumed my humble Chicago garb.

It's no wonder regular correspondents and British officers are obliged to wear canes. The wonder is that they don't use crutches.

We leave at nine to-morrow morning. This means that myself and puttees will have to get up at four.

Wednesday, September 5. With the British.

The major has a very good sense of the fitness of things. The room where I'm writing, by candle-light, is the best guest room in our château and was once occupied by the queen.

The rules of the household call for the dousing of down-stairs glims at eleven o'clock. After that you may either remain down there in total darkness or come up here and bask in the brilliant rays of a candle. You should, I presume, be sleepy enough to go right to bed, but you're afraid you might forget something if you put off the day's record till to-morrow.

I overslept myself, as they say, and had to get Mr. Gibbons to help with the puttees. The lower part of the breeches, I found, could be loosened just enough to make the knee area inhabitable.

"You look as if you had been poured into it"

We skipped breakfast and reached the station in a taxi without hitting anything. It was fifteen minutes before train time, but there wasn't a vacant seat in the train. A few of the seats were occupied by poilus, and the rest by poilus' parcels and newspapers. A Frenchman always gets to a nine o'clock train by seven-thirty. He picks one seat for himself and one or two on each side of him for his impedimenta. This usually insures him privacy and plenty of room, for it is considered an overt act even to pick up a magazine and sit in its place. Mr. Gibbons and I walked from one end of the train to the other and half-way back again without any one's taking a hint. We climbed into a carriage just as she started to move. There were six seats and three occupants. We inquired whether all the seats were reserved, and were given to understand that they were, the owners of three having gone to a mythical dining-car.

We went into the aisle and found standing room among the Australians and Canadians returning from their leave. One of the former, a young, red-headed, scrappy-looking captain, smiled sympathetically and broke open a conversation. I was glad of it, for it gave me an opportunity of further study of the language. I am a glutton for languages, and the whole day has been a feast. We have listened to six different kinds—Australian, Canadian, British, French, Chinese and Harvard. I have acquired an almost perfect understanding of British, Australian and Canadian, which are somewhat similar, and of Harvard, which I studied a little back home. French and Chinese I find more difficult, and I doubt that any one could master either inside of a month or so.

The red-headed captain remarked on the crowded condition of the trine. That is Australian as well as British for train. The Canadian is like our word, and the French is spelled the same, but is pronounced as if a goat were saying it. Lack of space prevents the publication of the Chinese term.

One of the captain's best pals, he told us, had just been severely wounded. He was a gime one, though even smaller than the captain. The captain recalled one night when he, the pal, took prisoner a boche lieutenant who stood over six feet.

Fritz was asked whether he spoke English. He shook his head. He was asked whether he spoke French. He lost his temper and, in English, called the entire continent of Australia a bad name. The captain's little pal then marched him off to the proper authority, to be questioned in English. On the way the captain's little pal made him take off his helmet and give it to him. This was as punishment for what Fritz had said about Australia.

Before the proper authority Fritz was as sweet-tempered as a bloody bear. This puzzled the proper authority, for making a boche prisoner is doing him a big favor.

"What iles you?" asked the authority when Fritz had refused to reply to any of a dozen questions. "You ine't the first bloody boche officer we've tiken."

Then Fritz bared his grievance. He didn't mind, he said, being a prisoner. The size of his captor was the thing that galled. "And for Gott's sake," he added, "make him give back my helmet."

The proper authority turned to the captain's little pal. "He's your prisoner," he said. "What do you want to do with the helmet?"

"Keep it, sir," said the captain's little pal.

And it will be used back in Australia some day to illustrate the story, which by that time will doubtless have more trimmings.

"But how about Fritz?" I asked. "When he gets home and tells the same story, he'll have nothing with which to prove it."

"He ine't agoin' to tell the sime story."

We were welcomed at our destination by a captain, another regular correspondent, and two good English cars. The captain said he was expecting another guest on this train, a Harvard professor on research work bent.

"I have no idea what he looks like," said the captain.

"I have," said Mr. Gibbons and I in concert, but it went over the top.

The professor appeared at length, and we were all whisked some thirty kilometers to a luncheon worth having. Afterward we were taken to the Chinese camp. Chinatown, we'll call it, is where the Chink laborers are mobilized when they first arrive and kept until their various specialties are discovered. Then each is assigned to the job he can do best. I was told I mustn't mention the number of Chinamen now in France, but I can say, in their own language, it's a biggee lottee.

They wear a uniform that consists of blue overalls, a blue coat, and no shirt whatever, which, I think, is bad advertising for their national trade. They brought shirts with them, it seems, but are more comfy without.

The minimum wage is three francs a day. Two-thirds of what they earn is paid them here, the other third given to their families in China. The system of hiring is unique. No names are used, probably because most Chinks have Sam Lee as a monniker, and the paymaster would get all mixed up with an army of Sam Lees. They are numbered and their finger prints are taken by an agent in China. He sends these identification marks to the camp here, and when the Chinks arrive they are checked up by a finger-print expert from Scotland Yard. This gentleman said there had been several cases where the Chinaman landing here was a ringer, some "friend" back home having signed up and then coaxed the ringer to come in his place, believing, apparently, that the plot would not be detected and that his profit would be the one-third share of the wage that is paid in China. The ringer's family would be done out of its pittance, but that, of course, would make no difference to the ringer's friend. The finger-print system serves not only to prevent the success of cute little schemes like that, but also to amuse the Chinks, who are as proud of their prints as if they had designed them.

We went into the general store, which is conducted by a Britisher. The Chinese had just had a pay-day and were wild to spend. One of them said he wanted a razor. The proprietor produced one in a case, and the Chink handed over his money without even looking at the tool. Another wanted a hat. The prop. gave him a straw with a band that was all colors of the rainbow. The Chinaman paid for it and took it away without troubling to see whether it fitted.

A block or so from the store we ran across two Chinks who had been naughty. Each was in a stock, a pasteboard affair on which was inscribed,

in Chinese, the nature of his offense. One of them
had been guilty of drinking water out of a fire
bucket. The other had drunk something else out of
a bottle—drunk too much of it, in fact. They
looked utterly wretched, and our guide told us the
punishment was the most severe that could be given:
that a Chinaman's pride was his most vulnerable
spot.

The gent who had quenched his thirst from the
fire bucket was sentenced to wear his stock a whole
day. He of the stew was on the last lap of a week's
term.

We talked with one of the Lee family through
an interpreter. We asked him if he knew that the
United States was in the war against Germany. He
replied, No, but he had heard that France was.

Just before we left the settlement a British plane
flew over it. A Chink who was walking with us
evidently mistook it for a Hun machine, for he
looked up and said: "Bloody boche!"

From Chinatown we were driven to the American
Visitors' Château, where gentlemen and correspondents from the United States are entertained. It's

a real château, with a moat and everything. The major is our host. The major has seen most of his service in India and China.

He said he was glad to meet us, which I doubt. The new arrivals, Mr. Gibbons, the Harvard professor and myself, were shown our rooms and informed that dinner would occur at eight o'clock. Before dinner we were plied with cocktails made by our friend, the captain. The ingredients, I believe, were ether, arsenic and carbolic acid in quantities not quite sufficient to cause death.

Eleven of us gathered around the festal board. There were the major and his aids, three British captains, one with a monocle. There was the Harvard professor, and the head of a certain American philanthropical organization, and his secretary. And then there were us, me and Mr. Gibbons and Mr. O'Flaherty and Mr. Somner, upstarts in the so-called journalistic world.

The dinner was over the eighteen-course course, the majority of the courses being liquid. I wanted to smoke between the fish and the sherry, but Mr.

O'Flaherty whispered to me that it wasn't done till the port had been served.

Mention was made of the Chinese camp, and there ensued a linguistic battle between the major and the Harvard professor. The latter explained the theory of the Chinese language. He made it as clear as mud. In the Chinese language, he said, every letter was a word, and the basis of every word was a picture. For example, if you wanted to say "my brother," you drew a picture of your brother in your mind and then expressed it in a word, such as woof or whang. If you wanted a cigar, you thought of smoke and said "puff" or "blow," but you said it in Chinese.

Mr. Gibbons broke up the battle of China by asking the major whether I might not be allowed to accompany him and Mr. O'Flaherty and one of the captains on their perilous venture to-morrow night. They are going to spend the night in a Canadian first-line trench.

"I'm sorry," said the major, "but the arrangement has been made for only three."

I choked back tears of disappointment.

The major has wished on me for to-morrow a trip through the reconquered territory. My companions are to be the captain with the monocle, the Harvard professor, the philanthropist, and the philanthropist's secretary. We are to start off at eight o'clock. Perhaps I can manage to oversleep.

Thursday, September 6. With the British.

I did manage it, and the car had left when I got down-stairs. Mr. Gibbons and Mr. O'Flaherty were still here, and the three of us made another effort to get me invited to the party to-night. The major wouldn't fall for it.

Mr. Gibbons and Mr. O'Flaherty motored to an artillery school, the understanding being that they were to be met at six this evening by one of our captains and taken to the trench. I was left here alone with the major.

We lunched together, and he called my attention to the mural decorations in the dining-room. It's a rural mural, and in the foreground a young lady is milking a cow. She is twice as big as the cow and is seated in the longitude of the cow's head. She reaches her objective with arms that would make Jess Willard jealous. In another area a lamb is conversing with its father and a couple of squirrels which are larger than either lamb or parent. In the lower right-hand corner is an ox with its tongue in a tin can, and the can is labeled Ox Tongue for fear some one wouldn't see the point. Other figures in the pictures are dogs, foxes and chickens of remarkable size and hue.

"We had a French painter here a few days ago," said the major. "I purposely seated him where he could look at this picture. He took one look, then asked me to change his seat."

The major inquired whether I had noticed the picture of the château which decorates the doors of our automobiles.

"When you go out to-morrow," he said, "you'll observe that none of the army cars is without its symbol. An artillery car has its picture of a gun. Then there are different symbols for the different divisions. I saw one the other day with three interrogation marks painted on it. I inquired what they meant and was told the car belonged to the Watts division. Do you see why?"

I admitted that I did.

"Well, I didn't," said the major, "not till it was explained. It's rather stupid, I think."

This afternoon an American captain, anonymous of course, called on us. He is stopping at G. H. Q., which is short for General Headquarters, his job being to study the British strategic methods. He and the major discussed the differences between Americans and Englishmen.

"The chief difference is in temperature," said the captain. "You fellows are about as warm as a glacier. In America I go up to a man and say: 'My name is Captain So-an-So.' He replies: 'Mine is Colonel Such-and-Such.' Then we shake hands and talk. But if I go to an Englishman and say: 'My name is Captain So-and-So,' he says: 'Oh!' So I'm embarrassed to death and can't talk."

" 'Strawnary!" said the major.

At tea time a courier brought us the tidings that there'd been an air raid last Sunday at a certain hospital base.

"The boche always does his dirty work on Sunday," remarked the American captain. "It's queer, too, because that's the day that's supposed to be kept holy, and I don't see how the Kaiser squares himself with his friend Gott."

I laughed, but the major managed to remain calm.

The American captain departed after tea, and the major and I sat and bored each other till the Harvard professor and his illustrious companions returned. They told me I missed a very interesting trip. That's the kind of trip one usually misses.

At dinner we resumed our enlightening discussion of Chinese, but it was interrupted when the major was called to the telephone. The message was from the captain who was supposed to meet Mr. Gibbons and Mr. O'Flaherty and take them to the trenches to spend the night. The captain reported that his machine had broken down with magneto trouble and he'd been unable to keep his appointment. He requested that the major have Mr. Gibbons and Mr. O'Flaherty located and brought home.

This was done. The disappointed correspondents blew in shortly before closing time and confided
to me their suspicion that the trouble with the captain's machine had not been magneto, but (the
censor cut out a good line here).

To-morrow we are to be shown the main British
training school and the hospital bases.

Friday, September 7.   With the British.

We left the château at nine and reached the training camp an hour later.

We saw a squad of ineligibles drilling, boys
under military age who had run away from home
to get into the Big Game. Their parents had informed the authorities of their ineligibility, and the
authorities had refused to enroll them. The boys
had refused to go back home, and the arrangement
is that they are to remain here and drill till they
are old enough to fight. Some of them are as
much as three years shy of the limit.

The drill is made as entertaining as possible.
The instructor uses a variation of our "Simon says:
'Thumbs up'." "O'Grady" sits in for Simon.

For example, the instructor says: "O'Grady says: 'Right dress.' Left dress." The youth who "left dresses" without O'Grady's say-so is sent to the awkward squad in disgrace.

Out of a bunch of approximately two hundred only two went through the drill perfectly. The other one hundred and ninety-eight underestimated the importance of O'Grady and sheepishly stepped out of line. The two perfectos looked as pleased as peacocks.

We saw a bayonet drill with a tutor as vivacious and linguistically original as a football coach, and were then taken to the bomb-throwing school. The tutor here was as deserving of sympathy as a Belgian. A bomb explodes five seconds after you press the button. Many of the pupils press the button, then get scared, drop the bomb and run. The instructor has to pick up the bomb and throw it away before it explodes and messes up his anatomy. And there's no time to stop and figure in what direction you're going to throw.

The Maoris were our next entertainers. The Maoris are colored gemmen from New Zealand.

They were being taught how to capture a trench.
Before they left their own dugout they sang a battle hymn that would make an American dance and
scare a German to death. They went through their
maneuvers with an incredible amount of pep and
acted as if they could hardly wait to get into real
action against the boche. Personally, I would have
conscientious objections to fighting a Maori.

Then we were shown a gas-mask dress rehearsal.
A British gas mask has a sweet scent, like a hospital. You can live in one, they say, for twenty-
four hours, no matter what sort of poison the lovely
Huns are spraying at you. We all tried them on
and remarked on their efficacy, though we knew
nothing about it.

We had lunch and were told we might make a
tour of inspection of the hospitals in which the
wounded lay. I balked at this and, instead, called
on a Neenah, Wisconsin, doctor from whose knee
had been extracted a sizable piece of shrapnel, the
gift of last Sunday's bomb dropper. This doctor
has been over but three weeks, and the ship that
brought him came within a yard of stopping a

torpedo. Neither war nor Wisconsin has any terrors left for him.

To-morrow we are to be taken right up to the front, dressed in helmets, gas masks, and everything.

Saturday, September 8. With the British.

Two machine loads, containing us and our helmets, masks, and lunch baskets, got away to an early start and headed for the Back of the Front. In one car were the Captain with the Monocle, the Harvard prof., and the American philanthropist. The baggage, the philanthropist's secretary, and I occupied the other. The secretary talked incessantly and in reverent tones of his master, whom he called The Doctor. One would have almost believed he considered me violently opposed to The Doctor (which I wasn't, till later in the day) and was trying to win me over to his side with eulogistic oratory.

The first half of our journey was covered at the usual terrifying rate of speed. The last half was a snail's crawl which grew slower and slower as we neared our objective. Countless troops, afoot and in motors, hundreds of ammunition and supply trucks, and an incredible number of businesslike and apparently new guns, these took up a healthy three-quarters of the road and, despite our importance, didn't hunch to let us pass.

When we sounded our horns to warn of our approach, the subalterns, or whatever you call them, would look round, stand at attention and salute, first the Captain with the Monocle, and then, when our car came up, me. Me because I was the only one in the second machine who wore a British officer's cap. I returned about three salutes, blushing painfully, and then threw my cap on the floor of the car and rode exposed. Saluting is a wear and tear on the right arm, and being saluted makes you feel slackerish and camouflagy, when you don't deserve it.

We attained the foot of the observation hill round noon, left our machines, and ate our picnic lunch, consisting of one kind of sandwiches and three kinds of wine. Then we accomplished the long climb, stopping half-way up to don helmets and masks.

Our guide told us that the boche, when not otherwise pleasantly employed, took a few shots at where we were standing to test his long-distance aim.

I wore the mask as long as I could, which was about half an hour. It was unpleasantly reminiscent of an operation I once had, the details of which I would set down here if I had time. Without it, I found, I could see things much more plainly. Through strong field glasses the British trenches were discernible. The German front line was behind a ridge, two hundred yards away—from the British, not us—and invisible. No drive was in progress, but there was the steady boom, boom of heavy guns, the scary siren, with a bang at the end, of grenades, and an occasional solo in a throaty barytone which our captain told us belonged to Mr. Trench Mortar.

The firing was all in one direction—toward the northeast. Fritz was not replying, probably because he had no breath to waste in casual repartee.

Convinced that our hill was a zone of safety, for this afternoon at least, I wanted to stay up there and look and listen till it was time to go home.

But our captain had arranged a trip to a sniping school, and our captain would rather have broken his monocle than have made the slightest alteration in the program for the day.

To the sniping school we went, and saw the snipers sniping on their snipes. It was just like the sniping school I had visited at the American camp, and I got pretty mad at our captain for dragging us away from a sight far more interesting. But he redeemed himself by having the major in charge show us real, honest-to-goodness camouflage, staged by an expert.

We were taken to a point two hundred yards distant from a trench system.

"Standing up in front of one of those trenches," said the major, "there's a sergeant in costume. He's in plain sight. Now you find him."

Well, we couldn't find him, and we gave up.

"Move, Sergeant!" shouted the major.

The sergeant moved and, sure enough, there he was!

"I had him spotted all the time," said The Doctor.

The major directed the sergeant to change to a costume of a different hue. When the change had been made we were required to turn our backs till he had "hidden" himself again. Again he was "in plain sight," and again we had to give up. Again he was ordered to move, and we saw him, this time in colors diametrically opposed to those of his first garb.

"I had him spotted all the time," said The Doctor.

The sergeant went through his entire repertory of tricks, but the rest must not be reported.

It occurred to me on the way back to our machines that some football coach could make a fish out of the defensive team by camouflaging his back field.

Our captain and the Harvard prof. climbed into the front car, leaving The Doctor, his secretary, and me to bring up the rear. The sec. sat with the driver; The Doctor and I in the back seat.

"How long have you been over here?" inquired The Doctor at length.

I told him.

"How many American soldiers are there in France?"

I told him.

After an impressive pause, he said:

"As a matter of fact, there are really—" And he increased my estimate by four hundred per cent. "Of course," he continued, "I have the right figures. They were furnished me by the Defense League before I left home. They naturally wouldn't give them to a writer because they don't want them published."

"And naturally," says I, "whenever they tell a writer anything in strict confidence, he rushes to the nearest Local and Long Distance Telephone Booth and gets Wilhelmstrasse on the wire."

"Oh, no," said The Doctor. "But a writer might think it was his duty to send the correct information to his paper."

"Did you ever hear of the censorship?" I asked him.

"There are ways of eluding it."

"And do you think all writers are that kind?"

He shrugged a fat shoulder.

"Not all, possibly a very few. But one never can tell the right kind from the wrong."

His guard was down, and I took careful aim:

"Do you think the Defense League used good judgment in entrusting that secret to you, when you spill it to the first irresponsible reporter you happen to run across?"

If I hadn't won this argument, I wouldn't repeat it.

Not until we reached our château did I realize why I had been so catty. I'd gone without my tea.

Sunday, September 9. Paris.

Mr. Gibbons and I this morning bade good-by to our genial hosts and were driven to the station at which we arrived last Wednesday. On the Paris-bound train I wondered audibly why the servants had given me that queer look before we left.

"Did you tip them?" asked Mr. Gibbons.

"Certainly!" I snapped.

"I'll bet I know," said Mr. Gibbons. "You probably packed your own suit-case."

He was right.

VI

HOW I DIDN'T DRIVE MAJOR BLANK'S CAR TO CAMP SUCH-AND-SUCH

Monday, September 10.   Paris.

THE American major who owns the car which Mr. Kiley drove down from Le Havre, whither it had been sent by the man who bought it in London for the American major—well, anyway, this American major, he's in the artillery camp at Such-and-Such, and he wants me to bring it down there for him. I've never handled, or, rather, footled one of the little birds, but it's something everybody should learn, like French and auction and how to swim. Besides, I want to see the artillery camp.   So I'm accepting the commission and intend to get busy to-morrow morning.

Tuesday, September 11.   Paris.

With an American pass and an order for the car, I taxied to the United States army garage, in the Quai Debilly.

"Avez-vous fixed vous with passes?" inquired a friendly inmate of the garage.

I showed him my American card.

"That isn't bien suffisant," he said. "You'll have to get a pink one to go through the French army zone."

I recalled then our troubles on a previous automobile trip and was glad he had spoken.

"Where do I go for that?" I inquired.

"Go," said he, "to the Préfet de Ligne du Communications." Or something like that.

"Où is il?"

"I think he's in the Rue François Premier."

"And is the car all right?"

"I guess so. Nos haven't looked at it yet."

I had let my taxi go, and twenty minutes were spent in getting another. It was another hour before we located the préfet.

A secretary examined my passport and American pass and took my dossier:

Name, nationality, birthplace, age, ancestry, real purpose in coming to France. Hair—black; forehead — high; eyes — brown; nose — prominent;

mouth—medium; chin—round; complexion—dark; height—six one and three-quarters. Sign here.

"Now," said the sec., "monsieur will avez to come across avec a photophie."

"I'm just out," I said. "I'd no idea I'd be so popular."

"Nos can issue no passes sans a photophie," says he, so out I went in search of a rapid-fire studio.

The driver pulled up in front of a gallery on the Rue de la Paix, where the artist promised to have six copies of my map printed by midi.

To kill time I rode back to Billy's rue.

"The car's on the blink," said my friend in French. "The connecting rod is lâche and some bearings are burned out. Besides, vous would be a rummy to partir on these tires."

"Comme beaucoup new ones do je need?"

"Just plain quatre," says he.

"Well," says I, "put them on and get busy avec the reparations. I want to start away before dark."

"Ah, oui," says he, "but we have no tires and we have no tools to make the reparations avec."

"Can't you get them?"

"Vous devoir get them yourself."

"Où?"

"At the branch factory of the ——," and he said the name of the car right out loud.

"Où est le branch factory?"

"Il est in un suburb—Le Vallois-Perret. The address is 6163 Rue Corneille."

"What tools are required?"

"Une roue-tirer et un offset clef à vis."

Which means a wheel puller and an offset wrench.

"And can je aussi tires get there?"

"Ah, oui."

It was noon, and my trusting driver and I returned to the studio on the Rue de la Paix. The pictures weren't fini. They never are.

"Take me to Maxim's," says I, "and we'll call it a half day."

After lunch I walked back to the studio. The pictures were not fini, but would monsieur rester? Monsieur would. Monsieur rested till fourteen o'clock, got six photophies that had him looking more than ever like a German spy, and taxied back to the Rue François Premier. The préfet's joint was closed.

I asked the driver how far it was out to Le Vallois-Perret.

"Come on," he said, and I climbed in, but "come on," in French, means "I don't get you," so I had to repeat the directions four or five times.

"Ah, oui," he said at last. "Le Vallois-Perret. Quatorze kilomet's."

"What is that in American money?"

"Come on," said the driver.

"Hotel Con-tin-en-tal," I said.

I'll tackle 'em afresh to-morrow morning.

Wednesday, September 12.   Paris.

The préfet's secretary approved my picture and gave me a beautiful salmon-colored pass. It is good for five days, which is plenty, as I will come back on the train.

At the city gates, en route to Le Vallois-Perret, my taxi and I were stopped and our essence measured. If we brought back more than we took out, we would have to pay taxes on the difference.

Quatorze kilomet's was a very conservative estimate of the distance, and it was nearly eleven when we reached Cornelia's rue and the branch factory.

An American heard my plea for four new tires, an offset wrench, and a wheel puller.

"It can't be done," he said. "All we do is own this place. But the French Government has taken it over and runs it."

"But this is a United States army car," I said, "and we're supposed to be allies of the French."

"Without special permission," said he, "you stand as much chance as if you were the Crown Prince."

"Where can I get special permission?"

"Your best bet is to see Captain Vandervelde. If anybody can fix it, he's the boy. You'll find him in the Passage de Haynau, Rue Croix Nivert."

"What number?"

"There is no number."

I thanked him, or perhaps I forgot to, and returned to my taxi.

"Passage de Haynau in Rue Croix Nivert," I said.

"Q'numéro?"

"There ain't none."

"Come on," demanded the driver.

"I told you there was no number. We'll just have to keep looking till we find it."

We convinced the guardian of the gate that we weren't trying to cheat on gasoline, and rolled into Rue Croix Nivert about thirteen o'clock. My chauffeur sat nonchalantly in his accustomed seat while I made a house-to-house canvass of Haynau's Passage. The last house was the right one. I knew it in an instant, for when I entered the corridor a French sentry popped up and placed the end of his bayonet within an inch of Nose-prominent.

"Captain Vandervelde," said I, making a short strategical retreat.

"Come on," said Frenchy without lowering his sticker.

A password was what he wanted, and Mr. Poincaré had forgotten to call me up and give me the correct one for the day. I produced a two-franc piece and held it out. The sentry withdrew his weapon, accepted the coin, and allowed me to pass.

"The word," I thought to myself, "must be Liberté, Egalité, Fraternité."

Captain Vandervelde was in and made me wait only half an heure, the while I thought more than once of yon taxi. Finally I was summoned to the inner office.

"What can je faire pour vous?" he inquired.

I told him I wanted an order on the —— branch factory for some tools and four new tires.

"Rien fairing on the tires," he said.

"Pourquoi?" I asked him.

"Orders pour tires must come from the Maison de la Guerre."

"Can you fix me for the tools?"

"Ah, oui. What tools voulez-vous?"

"Une roue-tirer et un offset clef à vis."

"Votre papers, s'il vous plaît."

I handed him passport, American pass, and salmon-pink card. He glanced them over, then began rummaging in a drawer. I knew what was coming —another dossier.

"Avez-vous une photophie?" he asked.

"Ah, oui," says I, and slipped him one of the remaining five.

He kept the dossier and photophie for the amusement of himself and progeny. He gave me only a mauve card which said I was entitled to one wheel puller and one left-handed offset monkey wrench.

I told my driver we had to hurry right back to Le Vallois-Perret. He looked crestfallen.

"Je have had no déjeûner," he said.

"Neither have je," I said, and climbed in.

Thursday, September 13. Paris.

Up early and to the garage. Delivered the tools. "Vous had better buy a tire pump," said my adviser.

"Je suppose," said I, "that I'll have to get an order for one from Papa Joffre."

"No," he said. "That's une chose vous can buy sans an order."

"Voulez-vous get to work on the car right away?"

"Ah, oui," says he.

I asked my chauffeur to take me to a maison du tire pumps. We found one on the Champs Elysées. Other things for sale in the store were watches and perfumery. I proceeded thence to French General Headquarters.

The gentleman authorized to sign orders for tires received me cordially and spoke English.

"Certainly," he said in answer to my request, "if the car is for an American officer. And what is the license number?"

I had to confess I didn't know.

"Well," said he, "you go to the garage and find out. Then come back and I'll give you the order."

I went to the garage to find out. There was no license.

"Où can je get one?" I asked my friend.

He gave me the address of the license bureau, on Rue Oskaloosa or something. The driver knew where it was.

Monsieur du License surprised me by asking for a picture and taking my description, which I could almost have rhymed by this time—

Hair jet black, but a paucity of it;
  Forehead high as the Eiffel tower;
Prominent nose, but it's mine; I love it;
  Eyes the brown of the pansy flower;
Medium mouth, not the best for kisses;
  Chin as round as a billiard ball;
Dark complected—Oh, Mister, this is
  Me, and I'm better than six feet tall.

"What est the numéro of the engine?"

"Four hundred and fifty-six thousand three hundred and four," I replied sans batting an eyelash.

He took it down and disappeared into an adjoining room. In a little while he returned with a license plate—second-hand to match the car.

I carried it along to display to the man at G. H. Q., as it is technically known.

"Où can I get the tires?" I asked.

"Anywhere, with that order," he said.

So I told the driver to go anywhere, and he misunderstood and took me everywhere. The tire maison he chose was as far away as he could drive without crossing the Swiss border.

"Now back to the United States garage," said I, and we arrived just as they were closing.

My friend told me the car had been "taken down." When I saw it I was convinced that the "taking down" had been accomplished with shrapnel.

"How many months will it take to put it together again?" I asked.

"Très few minutes," said the mechanic. "It will be all finished to-morrow midi."

"It looks all finished now."

"Avez-vous votre license?" he inquired.

I displayed it triumphantly.

"Ah, oui," he said. "But that's just the license for the car. Vous must aussi have a driver's license."

"Bonne nuit!" I yelped. "And what for?"

"C'est la loi," said he. "Everybody who drives in France must have one."

"How do you get it?"

"You'll have to go to the Chef de Traffic Police and pass the examination."

"How long does it take?"

"Très brief. Not more than une heure."

"Well, will you guarantee to have the car all ready when I come for it at noon to-morrow?"

"Je promise," he said, and I drove back to the hotel.

Oh, Major, wait till you see that taxi bill!

Friday, September 14.   Paris.

The traffic chief said that before he could examine me for a license I must show him my registration card from a regular police commissioner.   I had been told I ought to have one of those darn things, but had passed it up.   Now I was face to face with the necessity of acquiring the card and doing it quick.   The nearest station was only a few blocks away.   I found it jam-packed with people who looked as if they all worked in East St. Louis.   I flagged an attendant.

"I want to register," I told him.

"You'll be called when it's your turn," he said, and gave me a number.   It was 89,041.

"How long will I have to wait?"

He pondered.

"I think they're now in the twenty-thousands," he said.

Suddenly I bethought me of a document in my

pocket, a letter from the boss of the Maison de la Presse. I flashed it on him.

"Ah-h-h!" he sighed, and led me through the mob to the inner shrine.

In ten minutes I had my card. The commissioner didn't even want a picture, or nothin'. I plunged through the gang again and was stared at enviously. Some of the poor blokes have undoubtedly been waiting there since the Kaiser was forced into the war.

Again I appeared before the traffic chief. "Of course," he said, "I will have to examine your papers. And avez-vous une photophie?"

I came through.

"Now," I said, "we're fifty-fifty. You have one and I have one."

But he wasn't listening. He was rummaging for the deadly dossier.

"This," he said, when he had found one, "will have to be filled out."

"Yes," I replied, "I think I recall filling one out last time I was in France."

"This car belongs to an American army officer?"

"Ah, oui."

"What does he intend to do with the car?"

The temptation was strong to say he intended using it to tour the trenches. But it was no time to trifle.

"He expects to ride round the camp in it, sir. He is in one of the high commands and has to do a lot of inspecting."

"Do you know the traffic laws of Paris?"

"Ah, oui."

He didn't ask me what they were. But I could have told him. Any part of the street you like, with a minimum speed limit of forty miles on the straightaway and sixty-five miles round the corners.

"You are going to take the car right out of Paris?"

"Ah, oui."

"That's all," he said, and handed me a driver's license, horizon blue with saffron stripes.

I thanked him and bowed myself out of the place.

"From now on," I thought, "it's clear sailing."

The car was ready. I had in my mind's eye a near-by unfrequented street, where I was going to master the driving of it in ten minutes. Then I was going to shoot her up to the hotel, get my baggage and leave town.

"How about gas and oil?" I inquired.

"Oil, oui, but essence, no," said the mechanic.

"Well, throw in ten gallons," said I.

"Ah, but has monsieur an essence ticket?"

Monsieur never heard of it.

"Ah, then, monsieur can get no essence."

"Well for—" and monsieur used harsh words.

"Monsieur can easily obtain a ticket," said the guy when things had quieted down. "Monsieur's military passes will be suffisant."

"Where at?"

"At the Maison du Contrôle de l'Essence."

"And that is—?"

"Vingt sept, Rue Yaki Hula Hickey Dula."

"Is that as far away as it sounds?"

"Monsieur can go there and be back in une heure."

Monsieur crawled wearily into a taxi and started for Honolulu. The military passes did prove suffisant, and there was no trouble getting a fifty-gallon book at two francs per gal.

"I'll save time now," I thought. "I'll pick up my baggage on the way back to the garage."

So I told my driver to stop at the hotel. A telegram was waiting there for me.

"Hold car in Paris," it said. "Camp may be moved any day."

This blow fell at fourteen o'clock this afternoon. By half-past fifteen I had called up every steamship office and learned that the next boat for America would leave from England next Wednesday night. I am going to be aboard.

And now I have for sale, at auction:

> One pass through the French war zone.
>
> One pass good in the American camp.
>
> One driver's license.
>
> One book of essence tickets.
>
> One road map.
>
> One registration card.

I think I will leave the four tires and the offset

clef à vis and the wheel puller with the car. Also the car's license. The major is perfectly trustworthy. I only hope he doesn't get killed before my expense account reaches him.

VII

I START HOME, WITH A STOP-OVER
AT LONDON

Saturday, September 15.   Paris.

THE gentleman at the American Embassy, which
I visited late yesterday afternoon, spake truth
when he said it was some job to get away from
this place.

"If you want to leave on Sunday," quoth he,
"you'll have to rise early Saturday and keep going
all day.   See our consul first thing in the morning,
and he'll tell you all you have to do."

So I saw our consul first thing this morning.
In fact, I beat him to his office.   When he came in
he was cordial and unsuspicious, rare qualities in a
consul.   He stamped my passport "Bon pour se
rendre en Amérique par Grande Bretagne" and a
great deal more.

"Now," he said, "you'll have to be viséed by the

préfet de police and approved by the British Military Control. I don't know in what order. They change it every two or three days to keep you guessing."

I chose the British Control first and, of course, was wrong. But it took an hour to find this out.

There was a big crowd of us, and we were all given numbers, as in a barber shop of a Saturday night. But the resemblance to the barber shop ceased with the giving, for they called us regardless of number. A guinea sitting next to me was 42 and I was 18. He preceded me into the sanctum. And I got there ahead of No. 12, a British matron.

My session was brief.

"The police visé must come first," said the officer in charge.

Monsieur le Préfet has his office conveniently located about eight miles away from the Control, over the river. And he's on the fourth floor of a building constructed before the invention of the elevator. From behind an untrimmed hedge of black whiskers he questioned me as to my forebears, musical tastes and baseball preferences. Then he retired into chambers and presently issued forth with my passport, on which his stamp had been added to the beautiful collection already there. It says I'm Bon for a trip to Amérique par Angleterre, so I don't know whether I'm to go that way or through Grande Bretagne.

Thence back to Rue Napoléon Lajoie, and another long wait.

"Yes," said the officer when my turn came again, "the visé is all right, but where is your steamship ticket? You'll have to show that before we can pass you."

In order to show it I had to go and buy it, and in order to buy it I had to scare up some money, which is no mere child's play in Gay Paree these days. I called on four people before I found one who was touchable. With what he grudgingly forked over I hastened to the booking office and felt at home there, it being on Rue Scribe. There was a customer ahead of me—our president's youngest son-in-law.

"Do you know who that was?" said the agent excitedly when the young man had departed.

"Yes," I replied, "but we don't speak to each other."

"Now," said the agent, "I'm afraid I'll have to ask you a few questions. It's annoying, I know, but it's the war-time rule."

"Shoot," I told him. "I'm thoroughly used to being annoyed."

He ran through the familiar list and saved a new one for the wind-up.

"Why are you going to America?"

I could have spent an entire week replying to that, but even minutes were precious.

"Because it's where I live," proved satisfactory.

He apologized again for having to propound the queries, which shows he must be new on the job. The rest of them don't care whether you like it or not. I signed six or seven pledges, gave over the bulk of my borrowed fortune, and set out again with my ticket for the Rue Jacques Johnson. I got there just in time, for they close early on Saturday. Other days the poor devils have to work right through from ten to four.

The officer also wanted to know why I was going

to America. And he asked me at what hotel I would stop in London. I told him I'd never been there and knew nothing about the hotels.

"You must make a choice," he said. "We have to know your address."

"Is there one called the Savoy?"

"Yes."

"Well, let's say the Savoy."

"All right. You're to stay there, then, while you're in London, and you're to leave England on this ship Wednesday night. Otherwise you may have trouble."

I'll be surprised if I don't anyhow.

He decorated my passport with a heliotrope inscription, naming the port from which I'm to depart from France, the hotel in London, and my good ship, and sent me into the next room, where a vice-consul confirmed the military visé and relieved me of two francs.

The train leaves at seven to-morrow morning, and between now and then I have only to pack and to settle with the hotel. The former chore will be easy, for I possess just half as much personal property

as when I came.   Parisian laundries have commandeered the rest.

Monday, September 17.   London.

With tear-dimmed eyes, I said farewell to Paris
yesterday morning at the unearthly hour of seven.
There was not even a gendarme on hand to see me
off.

The trip from Paris to England is arranged with
the customary French passion for convenience.
They get you out of bed at five to catch the train,
which arrives in the port at noon.   The Channel
boat leaves port at ten o'clock at night, giving you
ten solid hours in which to think.   Not ten either,
for the last two are consumed in waiting for your
turn to be examined by the customs and viséed by
the Authorities du Exit.

Customs examination in this case is a pure waste
of time.   The gentleman only wants to know
whether you are trying to smuggle any gold money
out of France.   I'd like to see the departing guest
who has any kind of money left to smuggle.

The Authorities du Exit are seven in number.

They sit round a table, and you pass from one to the other until something has been done to you by each. One feels your pulse, another looks at your tongue, a third reads your passport right side up, a fourth reads it upside down, a fifth compares you with your photograph, a sixth inspects your visés for physical defects, and the seventh tries to throw a scare into you.

I got by the first six easily. No. 7 read both sides of the passport and then asked by whom I was employed. I told him.

"Where are your credentials?" he demanded.

"What do you mean, credentials?"

"You must have a letter from the magazine, showing that it employs you."

"You're mistaken. I have no such letter."

He looked very cross. But there were others left to scare, so he couldn't waste much time on me.

"I'll pass you," he said, "but if you come back to France again, you can't leave."

He and I should both worry.

But it does seem pathetic that the written and stamped approval, in all colors of the rainbow, of the Paris chief of police, the American consul, the British Military Control, the British consul, the French consul in New York, and nearly everybody else in the world, including our own Secretary of State, sufficeth not to convince a minor-league official that an innocent native of Niles, Michigan, isn't related by marriage to the Hohenzollerns.

On the dark deck of our Channel boat I had a 'strawnary experience. A British colonel to whom I had not been introduced spoke to me. He wanted a light from my cigarette. And when I had given it to him he didn't move away, but stayed right there and kept on talking.

"This is my first leave," he said (but in his own tongue), "since last March. Last year we were let off ten days every three months. Now we get twenty days a year."

"In 1918," said I, for something to say, "you'll probably have no vacation at all."

"In 1918," he replied confidently, "I believe we'll get three hundred and sixty-five days."

We settled the war in about half an hour. Then he asked me to join him in a Scotch and soda.

I was too gentlemanly to refuse. The bar, we ascertained, was closed. But we might find something in the dining-room. We did, but to make it legal we had to order biscuits, alias crackers, with the beverage. We didn't have to eat them, though. They looked to be in their dotage, like the permanent sandwiches which serve a similar purpose in certain blue-law cities of Les Etats Unis.

We settled the war all over again, and retired, the colonel politely expressing the hope that we would meet for breakfast.

The hope was not realized. I was through and out on deck by the time we docked at the British port, which was about six o'clock this morning.

No one was permitted to leave the ship till the customs officials and alien officers reported for duty, two hours later. Then we were unloaded and herded into a waiting-room, where an usher seated us. Another usher picked us out, four at a time, for examination, using a system of arbitrary selective draft. Mine was a mixed quartet, three gents and a female.

An officer looked at our passports and recorded

details of them in a large book. Another officer ran
the gamut of queries. And here I got into a little
mess by telling the truth. When he asked me what
countries I had visited, I told him France and
added "Oh, yes, and for one day Belgium." He
marked this fact on a slip of paper and sent me to
the next room. The slip of paper was there ahead
of me and I was once more a suspect.

The young lady of our quartet, a French girl,
was getting hers, and there was nothing for me to
do but listen. She had a letter from her mother to
a friend in England. The mother, it seems, had expected to come along, but had decided to wait three
weeks, "till the submarine warfare is over." The
officers were very curious to know where the mother
had picked up that interesting dope. The young
lady couldn't tell them. Well, she would not be
permitted to leave town till an investigation had
been made. She was led back into the waiting-
room and may be there yet for all I can say.

It was my turn.

"Are you an American?"

"Yes, sir."

"How long ago were you in Belgium?"

"About ten days ago."

"You told our officer outside that you had been in Paris five weeks."

"I told him Paris had been my headquarters and I'd made frequent trips in and out."

"How did you get to Belgium?"

"In an automobile."

"An automobile!"

"Yes, sir."

"What were you doing?"

"I was being the guest of your army."

A great light dawned upon them.

"Oh!" said one, smiling. "He means he was behind our lines, not theirs."

"I should hope so," said I.

"We're sorry to have misunderstood, sir," said the other, and I was escorted into the baggage-room. There my sordid belongings were perfunctorily examined, the official not even troubling to open my typewriter case nor a large ungainly package containing a toy for certain parties back home.

It was eleven o'clock when the examinations were

all over and we entrained for this town. I got off
at Waterloo and asked a taxi to take me to the
Savoy. It did and it drove on the left side of all
the streets en route. I'm still quaking.

Tuesday, September 18. London.

This morning I had my first experience with an
English telephone. I asked the hotel's operator to
get me the office of Mr. O'Flaherty, the American
correspondent I had met at the British front. In a
few moments she rang back.

"Are you there?" she said, that being London for
"Hello."

"Here's your number, then. Carry on," she said.

But carrying on was not so easy. There is a
steel spring on the combination transmitter-receiver
which you must hold down while you talk. I kept
forgetting it. Also I kept being electrically
shocked. But in the course of half an hour, with
the operator's assistance, I managed to convey to
the gentleman an invitation to call.

He came, and we started for the Bow Street police
station, where every visitor has to register within

twenty-four hours of his arrival. On the way we met Lew Payne, the actor, and Gene Corri, racing man and box-fight referee. Gene has friends among the bobbies, and I was put through in record time. They told me I'd have to go to the American consul for a visé and then come back for a second registration with the police. Mr. O'Flaherty opined that these jobs should be attended to at once, as my boat train was supposed to leave at nine to-morrow morning. Mr. Payne had a better idea.

"Let's telephone the steamship office," he said, "and find out whether your ship is really going to sail on schedule. They usually don't these days."

Mr. O'Flaherty did the telephoning, and, sure enough, the blamed thing's been postponed till Saturday night.

They asked me what I wanted to do next, and I said I'd like to pay my respects to George and Mary. But I hadn't let them know I was coming and they're both out of town.

We went to Murray's (pronounced Mowrey's) Club for lunch, though no one in the party was a member and you have to sign checks to get anything. Unlike most clubs, however, you pay cash simultaneously with signing the check, so we weren't cheating. I signed "Charles Chaplin" to one check and it went unchallenged.

Gene's two sons are in the British army, and the conversation was confined to them. I was told they were the best two sons a man ever had, but I knew better.

Murray's Club's orchestra is jazz and it gave Mr. O'Flaherty and me an acute attack of homesickness.

From there we rode to the National Sporting Club, of which Mr. Corri is king. He asked me to put on the gloves with him, but I'm not one of the kind that picks on people five or six times my age.

On Mr. Payne's advice, Mr. O'Flaherty and I purchased seats for a show called *Seven Day's Leave*, and that's where we've been to-night, we and another scribe, Mr. Miller of Dowagiac, Michigan, which, as every one knows, is a suburb of Niles.

The show is a melodrama with so many plots that the author forgot to unravel two or three hundred of them. Of the fifteen characters, one is the hero and the rest are German spies, male and female. The hero is a British officer. Everybody wanted to kill him, and so far as I could see there was nothing to prevent. But he was still alive when the final curtain fell. The actors made all their speeches directly to the audience, and many of them (the speeches) were in the soliloquy form ruled off the American stage several years ago.

In the last act the hero pretends to be blotto (British for spiflicated), so that, while he is apparently dead to the world, he can eavesdrop on a dialogue between two of the boche plotters and obtain information invaluable to England. The boches were completely deceived, which is more than can be said of the audience.

Wednesday, September 19.   London.

Took a walk past Westminster Abbey and Buckingham Palace and found they looked just like their post-card pictures.

It's almost as bad crossing streets here as in Paris. The taxis don't go as fast, but their habit of sticking to the left side keeps an American on what are known as tenterhooks.

Mr. O'Flaherty loomed up at noon and guided me to the office of a friend with money. This rara avis honored a check on an American bank, and now I think there's enough cash on hand to see me through. The only trouble is that my education in English money has been neglected and I don't know when I'm being short-changed. Constantly, I presume.

Living conditions here have it on those in Paris. There are no meatless days, and a hot bath is always available. The town is dark at night, but it's said to be not for the purpose of saving fuel, but as a measure of protection against air raids.

One of those things was staged last week and a bomb fell uncomfortably close to ye hotel. The dent it made in Mother Earth is clearly visible to the naked eye. I trust the bombers take every other week off. At dinner we met two American naval officers—a captain from Baltimore and a lieutenant from Rockford, which is in Illinois. What they told us was the most interesting stuff I've heard yet. But, like all interesting stuff, it's forbidden to write it.

Thursday, September 20.   London.

The American naval officers took me to luncheon. After luncheon I went to the American consul's where I was viséed. Thence to the Bow Street station for final registration.

This evening to *The Boy*, a musical play which could use some of the plot so prodigally expended in *Seven Days' Leave*. But the music isn't bad.

Friday, September 21.   London.

The naval officers and three of us holdup men had a bitter argument over the respective merits of Baltimore, Dowagiac, Rockford, Niles, and What Cheer, Iowa, of which Mr. O'Flaherty is a native, and, so far as I know, the only one. It was finally voted to award What Cheer first prize for beauty of name, Dowagiac for handsome young men, Niles for scenic grandeur, Rockford for social gaieties, and Baltimore for tunnels.

I wanted to do some work, but the rest of the

crowd seemed to think my room was open house for the balance of the day, and here they stuck despite all efforts to oust them.

To-night it was *Chu Chin Chow* at His Majesty's Theater. You have to keep going to theaters in London. They're the only places that are lit up.

Chu Chin Chow is a musical comedy based on *The Forty Thieves*, and the music, according to our unanimous opinion, is the best since *The Merry Widow*. I seem to have resigned as war correspondent to accept a position as dramatic critic. But, as Mr. O'Flaherty says, there's nothing to write about the war, and what you do write the censors massacre.

Our ship still thinks it's going to sail to-morrow night, and the train leaves at nine-thirty in the morning. I am to be convoyed to port by the captain and the lieutenant, whose holiday is over.

Saturday, September 22. In Bond.

We're anchored in the middle of the river and have no apparent intention of moving to-night. And everybody's out of cigarettes, and it's illegal to sell them while we're in bond, whatever that may mean. But I guess I'd rather be in it than in a spy's cell, which seemed to be my destination at one time to-day.

The United States naval gentlemen were down at the train early and commandeered the best compartment on it. They had saved a seat for me and an extra one on general principles. This was awarded to Mr. Hanson, one of the active members of the French Line conspiracy which caused my arrest in Bordeaux. I hope he's seasick all the way home.

On the trip up from London we scored a decisive verbal victory over the submarines and formulated the terms of peace. Captain Baltimore and Lieutenant Rockford said farewell at the Liverpool dock and started for wherever they were going. We found seats in the inspection room and waited. Mr. Hanson grew impatient at length. He flashed his passport, a diplomatic one, on the usher and was sent through in a hurry. Not so with this well-known suspect. I was among the last to be called. My passport, strangely enough, was approved, but the baggage examination was yet to come.

I found my four pieces—two containers of clothes and such, a typewriter, and the ungainly toy—and had them hoisted on to the inspection counter. The most curious man I ever knew went at them.

The typewriter came first.

"What is this?" he asked when he had opened the case.

"A typewriter."

"Where did you buy it?"

"In Chicago."

"What do you use it for?"

"For typewriting."

"Typewriting what?"

"Stuff for newspapers and magazines."

"Pretty handy, isn't it?"

"Very."

"Have you written any articles over here?"

"Yes."

"Where are they?"

"Some are in America by this time; others are in the censors' hands."

He wanted to know what publications I was connected with, and I told him. He allowed me to close up the typewriter case, and next launched an offensive against a young trunk. He examined my collars one by one and found them all the same size. He came upon a package containing five or six hundred sheets of blank copy paper. He inspected every sheet, holding many of them up to the light. He gave individual attention to each of the few bits of lingerie the Parisians had not considered worth keeping. He exhibited an amazing interest in my other suit. He fondled a beautiful gray sweater for fully five minutes. He went through a copy of the *Chu Chin Chow* score, page by page. I wondered he didn't sing it. Holding out only the blank paper, he repacked, and tackled the suit-case.

He counted the bristles in the tooth-brush. He found two French dictionaries and a French grammar and studied them for approximately one semester. He opened a nest of shirts and handkerchiefs and spread them out for a thorough review. I should hate to be a clerk in a gents' furnishing store and have him wished on me as a customer.

In the lower southeast corner he discovered an unopened box of shaving cream. As every one knows, this commodity comes in a tube, which is wrapped in transparent paper, and the tube, thus wrapped, is contained in a pasteboard box for protection or something. Old Curiosity opened the box and extracted the tube. He gazed at it through the wrapper, then removed the wrapper and stared at the nude tube.

"Where is this made?" he asked.

"In America. It comes out like a ribbon and lies flat on the brush."

Without comment, he reclothed the tube as well as he could in its mutilated wrapper, put it back in its box, and repacked the suit-case and shut it.

"Is that all you have?" he inquired.

"No," I said. "There's that big square package containing a toy."

Now about this toy. It's a complete but ridiculously impractical system of trenches. French soldiers of leaden composition are resisting a boche attack. Some are supposed to be throwing bombs. Others are fighting with bayonets. A few are busy with the trench guns. There are threads to represent barbed-wire entanglements and a few Huns en-

meshed in them.   Other Huns are prone, the victims
of the sturdy poilu defense.

The package had been opened for private ex-
hibition purposes in London, and as I am an awful
washout (British slang) at doing up bundles, I had
left the job to a chambermaid, who had discarded
the Parisian wrapping paper and used some on
which no firm name appeared.

Well, Mr. Question Mark now laboriously untied
the cord, took off the paper and the cover of the
box, and exposed the toy to the public and official
view. Instantly two British officers, whom we shall
call General Bone and Major Thick, flitted up to
the counter and peered at the damning evidence.

"What is this gentleman's name?" asked the general.

He was told.

"When did you make this thing?" he demanded.

"I didn't," said I.   "It was bought in a shop in
Paris."

"What shop?"

"You can't expect a person to remember the name
of a Parisian shop."

"Where is the firm's name on the paper?"

I explained that the original wrapper had been left in London.

"What is your business?" demanded the major.

"He's a correspondent," replied the inspector.

There ensued the old familiar cross-examination and the request for credentials I didn't have. The major asked the inspector whether I was carrying any papers.

"These," said the latter, and showed him the pile of blank copy sheets.

The major dived for it.

"It's all blank paper," said the inspector, and the major registered keen disappointment.

Next to my suit-case lay a bag belonging to a gentleman named Trotter, and on it was a Japanese hotel label. The general glimpsed it and turned on me. "When were you in Japan?" he asked.

I told him never.

"That piece isn't his," said the inspector. "It belongs to a Mr. Trotter."

"His first name is Globe," said I, but it was a wild pitch.

The major and the general had a whispered consultation. Then the former said: "Well, I guess he's all right. Let him go."

Some devil within me suggested that I say good-by to them in German, which I learned in our high school. I cast him out, and here I am, aboard ship, sitting still in the middle of the river. But I don't like being indefinitely bottled in bond and I appeal to you, Mr. Captain—

Take me somewhere west of Ireland where they know I'm not a spy,
Where nobody gazes at me with a cold, suspicious eye—
To the good old U. S. A.,
Where a gent can go his way
With no fear of being picked on forty thousand times a day.

VIII

BACK IN OLD "O SAY"; I START AN-SWERING QUESTIONS

Sunday, September 23.   At Sea.

A CARD on the wall of my stateroom says: "Name of Steward—Ring Once. Name of Stewardess—Ring Twice." If they'll give us deck space, we can put on a three Ring circus.

The ship was still in bond when we awoke this morning, and the cheerful rumor floated round that she sometimes remained in harbor a week before securing the Admiralty's permission to sail. But life-boat drill was ordered right after breakfast, and Ring Once told me this indicated a speedy de-parture. My boat is No. 9. It's a male boat except for one Japanese lady, Mrs. Kajiro Come-here-o, whose husband is also of our select crew.

Our drillmaster advised us to wear plenty of

heavy clothes till we were out of the danger zone, advice which it is impossible for me to follow. He said five blasts of the whistle would mean we were attacked. I think, however, that if I hear as many as three I'll start sauntering toward No. 9.

At noon we felt the throb of the engines, and forty minutes later we were out of bond and able to buy cigarettes.

Before luncheon we were assigned to our permanent seats. Naturally, I am at the captain's table, with a member of the House of Commons, a member of the House of Lords, a plain English gentleman, a retiring attaché of our embassy in London, his journalistic wife, and M. de M. Hanson of Washington and Peoria, his first name being Mal de Mer.

The talk to-day has been of nothing but submarines. The superstitious call attention to the fact that with us is a lady who was on the *Lusitania* when they torpedoed it. To offset that, however, we carry the president's youngest son-in-law, and surely there must be a limit to boche ruthlessness.

Monday, September 24. At Sea.

Our ship's cargo consists principally of titles, rumors and celebrities. Most of the titles belong to members of the British Commission which is coming over to talk food to Mr. Hoover. But there is also a regular baroness, round whom the young bloods swarm like bees.

The rumors deal with the course of the ship. Some folks say we are going up Iceland way; others that we are headed straight south; a few that we are taking the Kansas City route, and so on. The sun refuses to come out and tell us the truth, but there's a shore line in sight on our starboard, and Ring Once tells me it's the east coast of Ireland. That ought to indicate something about our general direction, but I don't know what. Of the celebrities, most of them are American journalists and other spies.

Tuesday, September 25. At Sea.

Between eight and nine every morning the bath steward, one Peter James, raps on the door and says: "Your bath is ready, sir." And you have to get up and go and take it for fear of what he'd think of you if you didn't. But it's pretty tough on a man who's just spent a month in France and formed new habits.

I stayed up all night playing bridge. I wanted to be sleepy to-day because I needed a hair cut and the best way to take 'em is unconsciously. The scheme was effective, and I didn't hear a word the barber said.

The three others in the bridge game were members of the British Food Commission. Britishers, I notice, are much slower at bridge than we are. They think a long while before they make a play; then they make the wrong play. I do the same thing with only half the expenditure of thought and time.

Wednesday, September 26. At Sea.

Captain Finch appeared at breakfast this morning. It was the first time he had honored us. His presence at table, I'm told, indicates that we are out of the danger zone.

On board we have a doctor, a D. D., who intends to lecture in America on the war. He happened to be at our table in the lounge this afternoon. Some one asked him if he had visited the front.

"Indeed, yes," he said. "I was there less than a month ago. The British entertained me and showed me everything. Why, one day they were taking me through the front-line trenches and I asked how far we were from the German front line. 'Hush, Doctor,' said one of the officers. 'The Germans can hear you talking now. They're only twenty yards away.'"

I asked him what part of the front he'd been on. He told me. It was exactly the same front I'd seen. But when I was there—and it was also less than a month ago—the depth of No Man's Land was two hundred yards, and there weren't any noncombatants batting round within sixty feet of a boche trench. No, nor a British trench either. I said as much right out loud, and I'm afraid I've spoiled his trip.

But honest, Doc, somebody was kidding you or else your last name is Cook.

Thursday, September 27. At Sea.

The sea was calm, the day was fair.
E'en Mal de Mer came up for air.

The voyage is getting sort of tiresome to us
Americans. For the British it's not so bad. Their
five meals per day break the monotony. They
breakfast from nine to ten, lunch from one to two,
tea from four to five, dine from seven to eight, and
sup from eleven on. But we can't stand that pace,
and have to waste a lot of time reading.

There is a ship library full of fairly good stuff,
but by far the most interesting matter is to be
found in a paper published on board every day.
Its title is *The Ocean Times and the Atlantic Daily
News*. It contains two pages of news, two pages
of editorial causerie, one of them in French, and
four pages of real hot stuff, such as "Softness and
Grandeur. A Brief Appreciation of a Delightful
Excursion in Norway"; "Chance Meetings. The
Long Arm of Coincidence and the Charm of Sur-
prise"; "The Introduction of Electric Tramways

into Cape Town." These essays and articles are boiler plate, as we journalists say, and we find them an excellent sedative.

The news is received by wireless from both sides of the ocean. To-day's dispatches from Washington fairly made our hair stand on end. One of them said: "The decision of the milk dealers here that they would not pay more than thirty-two cents per gallon for milk after October one was met by a counter-proposal on the part of the Maryland and Virginia Milk Producers' Association last night with an offer to fix the price at thirty-three and one-half cents per gallon instead of at thirty-five cents as originally planned." Another informed us that Brigadier-General Somebody, for three years assistant to the Major-General Commandant at the Marine Corps Headquarters, had been ordered to command the Marine Cantonment at Somewhere, Virginia. A person who fails to get a thrill out of that must be a cold fish. But I can't help wishing they'd let us know when and where the world series is to start.

It is announced that Doc Cook will preach at the ship's service Sunday morning. His text, no doubt, will be "Twenty Yards from the German Trenches."

Saturday, September 29. At Sea.

Captain Finch says we will reach New York Tuesday. But if they don't quit turning the clock back half an hour a day we'll never get there.

Sunday, September 30. At Sea.

The doctor preached, but disappointed a large congregation with a regular sermon.

After we had sung *God Save the King* and *America,* I came to my stateroom to work and immediately broke the carriage cord on my typewriter. I said one or two of the words I had just heard in church; then borrowed a screw driver from Ring Once and proceeded to dilacerate the machine. It took over an hour to get it all apart and about two hours to decide that I couldn't begin to put it together again.

I went on deck and told my troubles to Mr. Hollister of Chicago. Mr. Hollister was sympathetic and a life-saver. He introduced me to a young man, named after the beer that made Fort Wayne famous, who is a master mechanic in the employ of the Duke of Detroit. The young man said he had had no experience with typewriters, but it was one of his greatest delights to tinker. I gave him leave to gratify his perverted taste and, believe it or not, in forty minutes he had the thing running, with a piece of common binding twine pinch-hitting for the cord. Then I went entirely off my head and bought him wine.

Monday, October 1. Nearly There.

It's midnight. An hour ago we went on deck and saw the prettiest sight in the world—an American lighthouse. First we felt like choking; then like joking. Three of us—Mr. and Mrs. P. Williams and I—became extremely facetious.

"Well," said Mrs. Williams, "there's ' 'Tis of Thee.' "

"Yes," said her husband, "that certainly is old 'O Say.' "

I've forgotten what I said, but it was just as good.

The light—standing, they told me, on Fire Island—winked at us repeatedly, unaware, perhaps, that we were all married. I'll confess we didn't mind at all and would have winked back if we could have winked hard enough to carry nineteen nautical miles.

Ring Once was waiting at the stateroom door to tell me to have all baggage packed and outside first thing in the morning.

"I'll see that it's taken off the ship," he said. "You'll find it under your initial on the dock."

"What do you mean, under my initial?"

He explained and then noticed that my junk was unlabeled. I'd worried over this a long while. My French Line stickers had not stuck. And how would New Yorkers and Chicagoans know I'd been abroad? I couldn't stop each one and tell him.

The trusty steward disappeared and soon returned with four beautiful labels, square, with a red border, a white star in the middle, and a dark blue L, meaning me, in the middle of the star.

"Put those on so they'll stay," I instructed him. "There's no sense in crossing the ocean and then keeping it a secret."

Tuesday, October 2. A Regular Hotel.

M. de M. Hanson, looking as if he'd had just as much sleep as I, was in his, or somebody else's deck chair, reading a yesterday's New York paper, when I emerged to greet the dawn.

"I don't know where this came from," he said, "but it's got what you want to know. The series opens in Chicago next Saturday. They play there Saturday and Sunday, jump back to New York Monday and play here Tuesday and Wednesday."

"And," said I, "may the better team win—in four games."

We were anchored in the harbor, waiting for a pilot, that was, as usual, late. I was impatient but M. de M. didn't seem to care. He's wild about ocean travel so long as it's stationary.

Presently the youngest of the food commissioners, one Mr. Bowron, joined us. He asked the name of every piece of land in sight. We answered all his questions, perhaps correctly.

"That one," said M. de M., pointing, "is Staten Island. Of course you've heard of it."

"I'm afraid not," said Mr. Bowron.

"What!" cried Mr. Hanson. "Never heard of Staten Island!"

"The home of Matty McIntyre," I put in. "One of the greatest outside lefts in the history of soccer. He played with the Detroit and Chicago elevens in the American League."

Mr. Bowron looked apologetic.

"And in that direction," said Mr. Hanson, pointing again, "is Coney Island, where fashionable New York spends its summers."

"Except," said I, "the aristocratic old families who can't be weaned away from Palisades Park."

Mr. Bowron interviewed us on the subject of hotels.

"There are only two or three first-class ones," said Mr. Hanson. "The Biltmore's fair. It's got elevators and running hot water."

"But no electric lights," I objected.

"Oh, yes," said Mr. Hanson. "They put in electricity and set the meter the week we left."

Breakfast was ready, and for the first time on the trip Mr. Hanson ate with a confidence of the future. For the first time he ordered food that was good for him. Previously it hadn't mattered.

When we went back on deck, the world's largest open-face clock was on our left, and on our right the business district of Pelham's biggest suburb. And immediately surrounding us were Peter James and Ring Once and the lounge steward and the deck steward and the dining-room stewards—in fact, all the stewards we'd seen and a great many we hadn't.

"We're trapped," said Mr. Hanson. "Our only chance for escape is to give them all we've got. Be ready with your one-pounders and your silver pieces."

At the end of this unequal conflict—the Battle of the Baltic—Rear-Admiral Lardner's fleet was all shot to pieces, most of them the size of a dime, and when Mr. Brennan of Yonkers announced that his car would meet the ship and that he would gladly give me a ride to my hotel I could have kissed him on both cheeks. It took my customs inspector about a minute to decide that I was poor and honest. The baroness, though, when we left the dock, was engaged in argument with half a dozen officials, who must have been either heartless or blind.

Mr. Brennan's chauffeur drove queerly. He insisted on sticking to the right side of the street, and slowed up at busy intersections, and he even paid heed to the traffic signals. In Paris or London he'd have been as much at home as a Mexican at The Hague.

The hotel gave me a room without making me tell my age or my occupation or my parents' birthplace. The room has a bath, and the bath has two water faucets, one marked hot and one marked cold, and when you turn the one marked hot, out comes hot water. And there's no Peter James around to make you bathe when you don't feel the need.

The room has a practical telephone too, and pretty soon I'm going to start calling up acquaintances with kind hearts and good cooks. The first who invites me to dinner is in tough luck.

Friday, October 5.   Chicago.

"Miner" Brown, the great three-fingered pitcher, used to be asked the same questions by every one to whom he was introduced.   As a breath-saving device he finally had some special cards printed. On one side was his name.   On the other the correct replies :

1. Because I used to work in a mine.
2. It was cut off in a factory when I was a kid.
3. At Terre Haute, Ind.
4. Rosedale, right near Terre Haute.
5. Not a bit.

When he left home in the morning he was always supplied with fifty of these cards, and sometimes he got rid of the whole supply before bedtime.

I departed from New York Wednesday night. Our train picked up the New York Baseball Club at Philadelphia.   I was acquainted with about fifteen of the twenty (odd) athletes.   Every one of the fifteen, from Mr. Zimmerman down, shot the same queries at me.   Every person I've encountered here at home too, and usually in the same order :

1. How'd you like it over there?

2. Did you see any subs?

3. Did you see any fighting?

4. Could you hear the guns?

5. How close did you get to the front?

6. Did you see any American soldiers?

7. How many men have we got over there?

8. How are things in Paris?

9. Were you in England?

10. How are things in London?

11. Were you in any air raids?

12. How long is it going to last?

Now truth may be stranger than fiction, but it's also a whole lot duller. Most of my answers have very evidently bored my audiences to the point of extinction. Yet I hesitate to start weaving the well-known tangled web. I'd be bound to trip in it sooner or later. Last night, in desperation, I drafted a card along the line of Mr. Brown's. But it lacked wallop, as you can see for yourself.

1. Oh, pretty well.

2. No.

3. A little.

4. Oh, yes.

5. A mile and a half, on the observation hill.

6. Oh, yes.

7. That's supposed to be a secret.

8. Pretty gay.

9. Yes.

10. All right, so far as I could see.

11. No.

12. I don't know.

THE END